Emergency repairs for historic buildings

English Heritage

Emergency repairs for historic buildings

Eleanor Michell

commissioned by the Historic Areas Division of English Heritage

published in conjunction with Butterworth Architecture

1988

Published 1988 by English Heritage
Fortress House, 23 Savile Row,
London W1X 2HE

ISBN 1 85074 227 8

Emergency repairs for historic buildings has been written by Eleanor Michell in collaboration with English Heritage for general use, but the opinions expressed remain those of the author and may not necessarily be taken as indicating the opinion of English Heritage in any particular case.

Layout and design by Frank Gardiner of English Heritage Academic and Specialist Drawing Office

Contents

1 Introduction

1.1 Emergency repairs for historic buildings 8
1.2 Historic buildings at risk 8
1.3 Basic aids for conservation officers 11
1.4 Condition surveys 12
1.5 Causes of deterioration in historic buildings 12
1.6 Grants for repairs 13
1.7 Legislation for urgent repairs 13
1.8 The use of the legislation 14
1.9 Historic buildings preservation trusts 15

2 Temporary repairs and the care of unused buildings

2.1 A building under temporary repair 16
2.2 Assessment 17
2.3 Recording and conserving 17
2.4 Safety 18
- 2.4.1 The stability of the building 18
- 2.4.2 Public safety and access 21
- 2.4.3 Protection from traffic 21

2.5 Security 23
- 2.5.1 Assessing security 23
- 2.5.2 Assistance with security 23
- 2.5.3 Deterring vandals 24
- 2.5.4 Physical protection 25
- 2.5.5 Fire precautions 29
- 2.5.6 Intruder alarms 30
- 2.5.7 Graffiti 30

2.6 Excluding water 31
- 2.6.1 Roofs 31
- 2.6.2 Rainwater systems 33
- 2.6.3 Rising damp 34
- 2.6.4 Drying out and ventilation 35
- 2.6.5 Cocooning 36
- 2.6.6 Screening of openings 37
- 2.6.7 Water supplies 38

2.7 Organisms 38
- 2.7.1 Fungi 38
- 2.7.2 Woodboring insects 39
- 2.7.3 Birds 40
- 2.7.4 Harmful growths 40

2.8 Special features 41
- 2.8.1 External enrichments 41
- 2.8.2 Plasterwork and rendering 42
- 2.8.3 Wall and turret clocks 42
- 2.8.4 Organs 44

2.9 External appearance 44

3 Temporary uses for historic buildings

3.1 The need for temporary uses 46
3.2 Obtaining vacant possession when required 46
3.3 Payments and obligations for temporary use 46
3.4 Care of valuable features 47

3.5 Short-life housing 47
3.6 Temporary shops 47
3.7 Industrial and commercial uses 49
3.8 Community uses 50

4 Examples of emergency repair

Case study 1 The Lamb Inn, Wallingford, Oxfordshire 51
Damage caused by ineffectual emergency repairs
Case study 2 5–7 Elder Street, Spitalfields, London 56
Short term emergency repair
Case study 3 Arkwright House, Preston, Lancashire 60
First aid repairs by volunteers
Case study 4 Houses in Gillygate, York 63
Saving an historic street
Case study 5 Rock Hall, Farnworth, Bolton, Lancashire 73
The problems of an isolated historic building
Case study 6 113–115 Bath Road, Cheltenham, Gloucestershire 77
The determination of the planning authority saves a Regency elevation
Case study 7 Warehouse, Liverpool Road Station, Manchester 81
The problems of a very large historic structure
Case study 8 Brandling Station, Felling, Gateshead 85
A tiny unwanted building with historic associations
Case study 9 The Royal Naval Asylum, Penge, London 89
Permanent emergency repairs solve an intractable problem
Case study 10 Island Warehouse, Ellesmere Port, Cheshire 95
Long-term dedication by volunteers
Case study 11 Maw's Tileworks, Ironbridge, Shropshire 102
Irreparable damage in one year of neglect
Case study 12 32 Heathcoat Street, Nottingham 109
Permanent emergency repairs to a valuable street elevation

5 Aspects of the case studies

5.1 Choice of buildings 113
5.2 First steps 113
5.3 The cost of emergency repairs 114
5.4 The quality of the emergency repairs 114
5.5 Achievements 114

Appendix 116

Acknowledgements 119

Index 120

1 Introduction

1.1 Emergency repairs for historic buildings

Emergency repairs are needed for a building in such poor condition that if action is not taken the building, or its valuable features, might deteriorate until repair would no longer be feasible on either practical or financial grounds. These buildings are very often unoccupied and, until a new use can be found for them, face an uncertain future.

Emergency repairs could consist of permanent or temporary work. Permanent work should always be carried out according to the best historic buildings practice; these repairs, being well documented elsewhere, are not covered in this book. Temporary work is a second best made necessary by lack of money but having the advantage of speed. In an emergency this is sometimes the most important factor as decay spreads very quickly, especially in empty buildings. Chapter 2 of this book provides guidelines for temporary repair which indicate that even this work should be the best quality of its kind.

Historic buildings are here defined as listed buildings in England together with those which, although unlisted, add an historical dimension to their environment. This book mainly relates to the great majority of these buildings, rather than to major country houses, historic engineering works, or ancient monuments.

1.2 Historic buildings at risk

Owners are responsible for the repair of their buildings but local authorities have powers to encourage and enforce action when an historic building is at risk.

For the action to be effective the local authority needs the skill and experience of a team with architectural, planning, and administrative skills, and the ability to inspire enthusiasm in others. The members of the team need to have particular knowledge of historic building construction and be able to call upon the advice of architectural historians, archaeologists, and people with special expertise in such subjects as medieval carpentry, geology, or stone masonry. A team of this kind could be, and sometimes is, set up by a large council or the council of an historic town with perhaps 1000 to 4000 listed buildings; it could scarcely be justified by a district council with, say, 500 listed buildings.

The obvious answer to this problem is for all the district councils who do not have the requirements or the resources for a specialist team to cooperate with their county council wherever such a team exists at county level. Each district planning officer needs the services of a conservation officer and there should be the fullest cooperation with the county wherever there is the prospect of gaining specialised support. Such arrangements already operate in some counties and have proved very effective.

City of

Directorate of Development Services

Historic Buildings Record

File Refs			
Map Refs	SE 1532 SE		
Listing Serial No.	45/678, 679	Date Listed	21.12.77.
Grade	II	G.V. ✓	Other Status
Cons: Area	Little Horton Lane		

Howard Street (South)
Nos. 1-33 (odd)

Howard Street (North)
Nos. 4-32 (even)

Post Code		Tel. No.	

Public Ownership: H

Building At Risk: ★

Description "c.1850 Terraces of sandstone brick 2 storeyed houses. Slate roof with corniced chimneys. Stone bracket eaves cornice. Plain revealed sash windows. Nos. 1 to 19 have paired or single doorways with architrave surrounds and cornice on consoles, intervening archivolt arched passage entries. Included for interest as unaltered small town house terrace at the beginning of the mid century building boom."

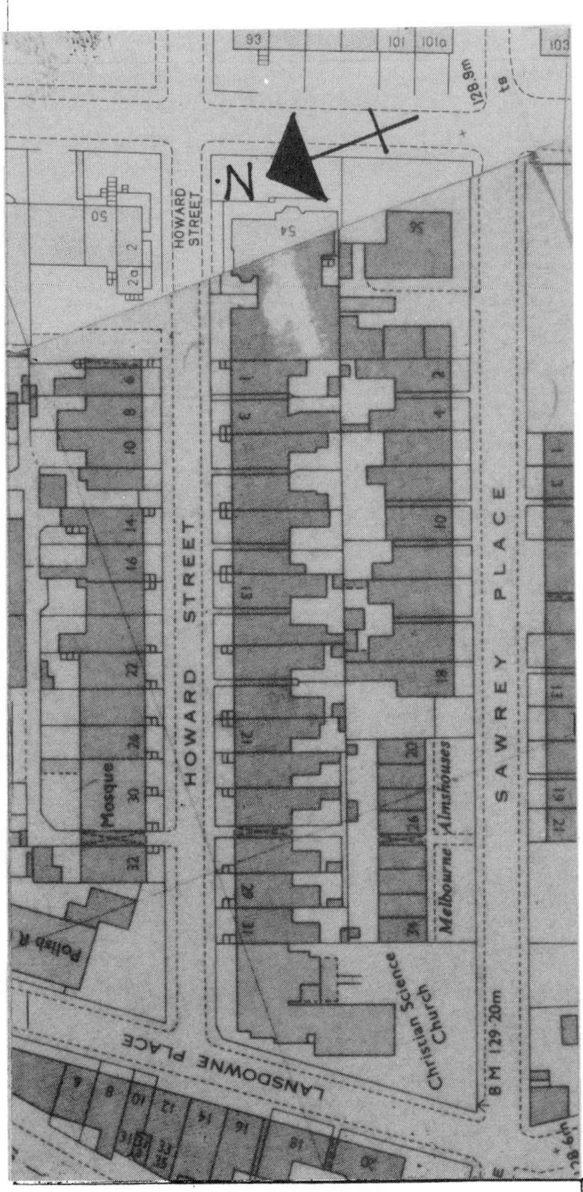

Scale of Map Cutting	1:1250	Date of Photograph	Upper 1978 Lower 14.2.82.
Background Material		Photographic Refs.	

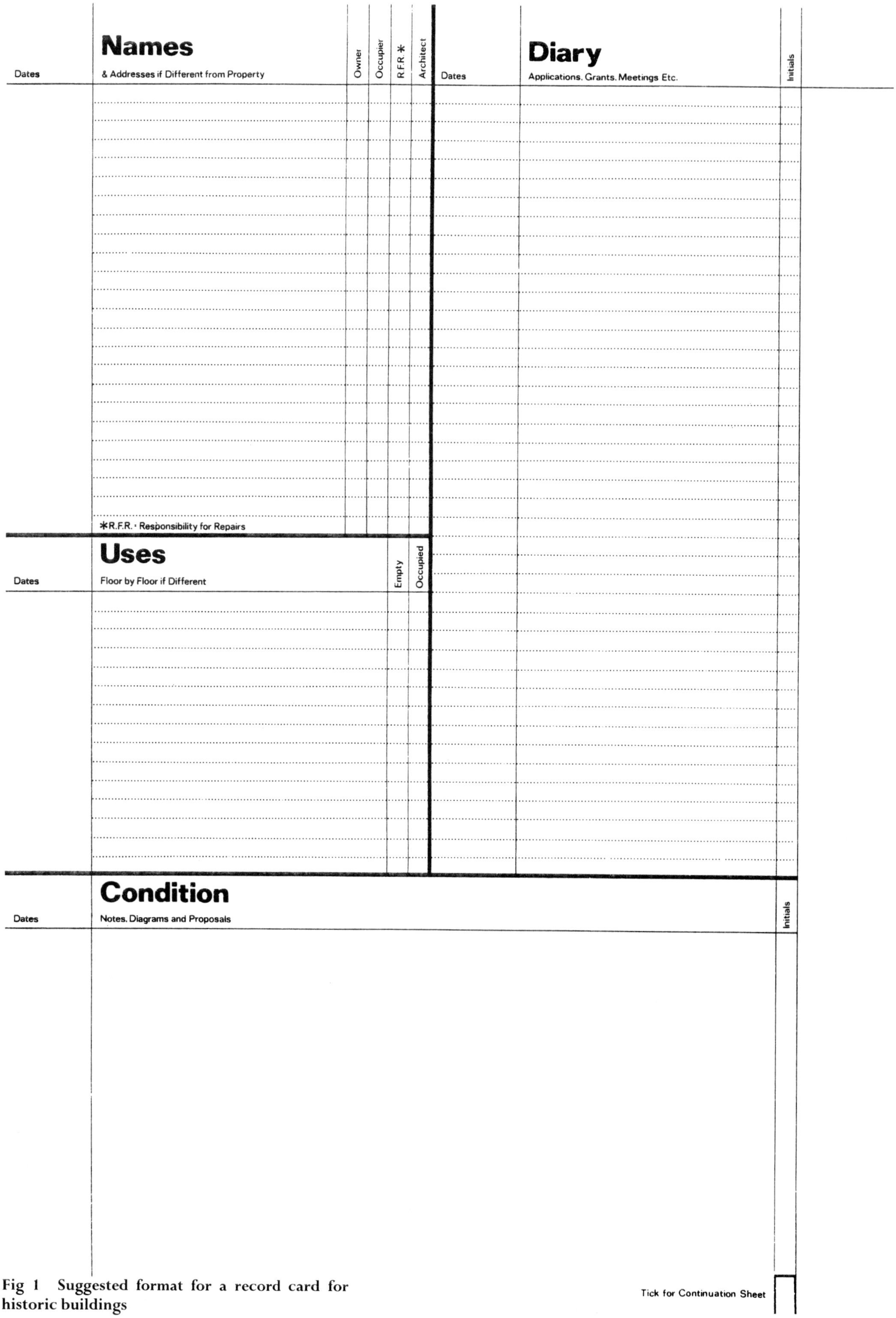

Fig 1 Suggested format for a record card for historic buildings

1.3 Basic aids for conservation officers

To prevent the deterioration of historic buildings and, when necessary, to ensure their repair, the conservation officer needs the following aids:

- A record system which identifies the historic buildings in the area and is designed to allow extra information to be inserted about each building in the course of daily work. An A4 size card for each building with historical information on one side and updated information on the other could meet this need and a suggested format is shown (Fig 1).

- A list of historic buildings at risk and a conspicuous removable tabbing system to mark these buildings in the record. The list would be compiled by obtaining information from such sources as building inspectors, amenity societies, estate agents, community groups, and preservation trusts, and through the day to day work of the conservation officer. A method of compiling a register of buildings at risk which could be used nationally is being developed by English Heritage.

Fig 2 Preston Street, Bradford, bought for demolition and subsequently listed as an early example of cluster block houses

- A list of historic buildings owned by the authority and a conspicuous tabbing system to mark them in the record. These buildings need particular attention in order that they should provide an example of good maintenance to other owners. If the record cards are illustrated with clear photographs they can be used to present information about the merits and the condition of the buildings to the committees which are responsible for their upkeep. The object would be to ensure that emergency repair was never needed; however, historic buildings are sometimes bought for demolition in favour of new schemes which are then abandoned (Fig 2). In these circumstances authorities could demonstrate the efficacy of emergency repairs well done, whether the work is permanent or temporary.

1.4 Condition surveys

Condition surveys of groups of historic buildings may be undertaken when a Town Scheme is under consideration, or when a repairs campaign or a scheme to persuade adjoining owners to solve their problems by cooperating with each other is planned. Condition surveys may also be needed to formulate planning policies, and they incidentally identify buildings to be added to the list of historic buildings at risk. They provide information to enable repairs to be put in hand in time and thus avoid the later need for emergency action.

1.5 Causes of deterioration in historic buildings

The primary cause of deterioration is neglect by the owner. The most common causes of this neglect are an inability to find an appropriate user, and buying a building for demolition. The most widespread physical cause of decay, resulting from this neglect, is water penetration setting up rot and infestation, the effect of which is swiftly cumulative and ultimately leads to collapse.

The second most prevalent cause of decay is vandalism in empty buildings.

Other causes of deterioration are less common but can be listed as follows:

- Destructive alterations for new uses.

- Poor local building materials, for example a soft stone or the use of timber for the sole plate.

- Bad workmanship especially in repairs.

- Atmospheric exposure (especially in coastal areas) and frost damage.

- Structural settlement caused, for example, by mining subsidence or shrinkable clays, or by the erosion of structural items by damp.

- Fire damage, whether deliberate or accidental.

1.6 Grants for repairs

A grant, however small, can be a tremendous encouragement to an owner to carry out repairs. Some of the grants now available are as follows:

- Grants from English Heritage for outstanding buildings. Normally only Grade I or II* buildings are eligible to be considered as outstanding.

- 'Town Scheme' grants which provide 40% of the cost of approved repairs. These are for selected buildings, both listed and unlisted, within certain conservation areas, and are made from annual budgets established jointly by English Heritage and the relevant local authorities.

- 'Section 10' conservation grants from English Heritage for projects within certain conservation areas.

- Historic Building grants from local authorities towards the repair of buildings which they consider to be important in their areas. The building need not be listed to qualify.

- Grants from English Heritage to local authorities towards the cost of acquiring historic buildings whose repair cannot be achieved in any other way.

- Other grants from public funds which are fully described in the English Heritage *Directory of public sources of grants for the repair and conversion of historic buildings*.

- Grants from charitable trusts, the criteria for which are described in the *Directory of Grant-Making Trusts*.

1.7 Legislation for urgent repairs

Listed buildings are protected against deterioration in two ways, as follows:

- Under 'Section 101' (Town & Country Planning Act 1971 as amended) the owner of an unoccupied or partly occupied listed building can be given seven days' notice by the relevant authority to carry out such works as are considered urgently necessary for the preservation of the building. If no action is taken, the authority can undertake the work itself. The cost can then be recovered from the owner, who is entitled to appeal on the grounds that the amount specified in the notice is unreasonable, that its recovery would cause hardship, or that some or all of the works were unnecessary. These provisions can sometimes be applied to unlisted, unoccupied buildings in a conservation area.

- A listed building can be compulsorily acquired when it is not being properly preserved. Such action can only be taken after the serving of a Repairs Notice (under Section 115, T&CP Act 1971 as amended); this gives the owner at least two months in which to take suitable steps towards carrying out those works which the authority considers reasonable and necessary.

1.8 The use of the legislation

The members of a conservation team often achieve their objects by means of friendly persuasion and sound advice rather than by invoking the legislation. At the same time, the mere existence of the legislation, as explained by the conservation officer, often convinces the owner of a deteriorating building to put the repairs in hand, or to sell to someone better able to do so.

When persuasion fails, the authority may be reluctant to serve a notice. If they are likely to be carrying out the repairs themselves they fear that they may not recover the cost, as the owner may claim that their requirements were unnecessary or unreasonable. Chapter 2 below is suggested as the basis of a yardstick of minimum repair which could be referred to by all parties.

Authorities have also been reluctant to undertake compulsory acquisition, particularly if a new user cannot be found and if they lack the personnel, the expertise, or the funds to follow through with repair, conversion, and resale. It is here that historic buildings preservation trusts can have a vital role to play.

Fig 3 1–3 Green Hill, Wirksworth, before repair

Fig 4 1–3 Green Hill, Wirksworth, after rescue by the Derbyshire Historic Buildings Trust; Architects: Derek Latham Associates

1.9 Historic buildings preservation trusts

See Appendix entry 1

Such trusts can give the authority confidence to issue Repairs Notices by undertaking to buy buildings if necessary. It can relieve the authority of the embarrassment of owning a deteriorating building which it does not want or need. Preservation trusts operate revolving funds, often using loans from the Architectural Heritage Fund, and are frequently helped by support from English Heritage and the county council. Their purpose is to buy, repair, and resell historic buildings and their courage and determination deserve every possible support (Figs 3 and 4).

2 Temporary repairs and the care of unused buildings

2.1 A building under temporary repair

This chapter is concerned with those historic buildings which are neglected, derelict, or in need of emergency repair, as well as with those which are unused, lacking proper maintenance, or otherwise at risk. The general care of unoccupied buildings is covered in addition to temporary repairs.

Temporary repair is never better or, in the long run, cheaper than permanent repair because, by definition, it will have to be replaced. But when a listed building is unused, its future uncertain, and the money for permanent work unavailable, there is an absolute minimum level of care which it deserves to receive. This includes protection, temporary repair, and measures to facilitate permanent repair when this becomes possible.

There are other circumstances where the future of a building is virtually assured but repair work is deferred while funds are raised or a full scheme is prepared. In these cases the building will need temporary protection and most of the information in this chapter will be applicable.

The appearance of a listed building under temporary repair is of the utmost importance. Although temporary, the repairs may have to be maintained for many years, and meanwhile the building must protect its valuable internal features, contribute to its environment, and give pleasure to those who look at it (Fig 5). A listed building is one to whose future we are legally committed for well-defined

Fig 5 Harden Old Hall, St Ives, Bingley, in 1981, empty but permanently reroofed pending a new use; meanwhile it plays its part in an extensive group of interesting buildings

reasons which are concerned with appearance and history. To allow those reasons to be set aside, even temporarily, is to begin a series of incidents which jeopardise the future of the building and frequently those around it.

The danger of specifying temporary repairs or minimum standards is that by default they may gradually be thought of as permanent repairs and become acceptable. Therefore, whatever the circumstances of temporary repair, the owner or authority ordering the work and the architect or surveyor specifying it should record its temporary nature and arrange methods of following it up with regular inspections and permanent repairs.

This chapter has two uses: first, it provides information on ways of arresting decay when absolutely nothing better is possible; second, it provides guidelines for local authorities as to the minimum care which should be given to an unused listed building.

2.2 Assessment

An empty or neglected historic building presents the owner with many problems such as possible future uses, the relative importance of different historic aspects of the building, the kind of repairs needed, and whether a condition or feasibility study would be advisable. On all these matters the local authority should be in a position to offer free advice, particularly if it employs a conservation officer.

Even if the immediate prospect can only be one of temporary repair, it is as well to have a choice of long-term objectives; if the owner hopes to sell or lease the building to a new user, it is an advantage to be able to present simple but attractive plans of possible conversions. An architect should be asked to undertake this work, and to make a careful survey of the building so as to reveal the most urgent needs for protection or repair.

2.3 Recording and conserving

Recording the building before any alterations are made is vital. This could be achieved in just a couple of pages with a small drawing and a few photographs, or it may be necessary to prepare a full report accompanied by measured drawings and a photographic survey. The information obtained should include details of the origins and history of the building; these are needed so that the development of the building throughout its life may be understood, and in order to assess the relative importance of existing features.

If any dismantling is carried out at temporary repair stage successive photographs will be needed as parts of the structure are removed. Much higher levels of recording are available, through the use of photogrammetry and archaeological interpretation; these may be necessary for sufficiently important historic structures, especially if further deterioration cannot be prevented.

It is especially important to record features of the building which are weathering badly or which are likely to be damaged before full

Fig 6 These garlanded corbels broke into pieces when the rotted bay was taken down for rebuilding; enough pieces were saved and reassembled to make a mould for replacements

repair is possible. The temporary work should protect them in position, and only if they are unacceptably loose or vulnerable should they be removed and stored. These objects should be labelled and placed in open boxes or stacks in one room in the building; items that are removed elsewhere are frequently lost by the time repairs begin. Specially recorded arrangements will have to be made for the storage elsewhere of valuable items which would attract thieves. It is unwise to store anything in the basement, where damp or even flooding may be worse hazards than theft; nor should the roof space be used with the possibility of exposure to birds and leaks.

The types of loose items which could be stored are stone, stucco, composition, or plaster mouldings, wood or cast iron balusters, broken sections of handrails, loose ironmongery, loose wall, floor, or hearth tiles, fireplace kerbs, shutters, lettering, notices, industrial archaeological items, coloured glass, crown glass (slightly bowed panes), unstable chimney pots, steps, doors, panelling, and so on. These items, however worn, can be reinstated or copied when the time comes to repair the building (Fig 6). If they are left lying about they may be lost or trodden on; they may even survive in place for years, until the contractor moves in for full repair and simply clears them away or breaks them.

2.4 Safety

2.4.1 The stability of the building

An historic building has normally, by definition, already been standing for a long time and the behaviour of the building itself over the years provides factual evidence for its condition which must be considered alongside any theoretical calculations. In considering the safety of an historic building the factors which will cause concern are ground movements, ill-considered alterations which have weakened the structure, and deterioration of structural members usually caused by water penetration or beetle attack. Excessive superimposed loads could also obviously cause trouble; in the case of temporary repairs existing loads can be carefully removed and new ones avoided.

If dangerous movements are suspected the building control officer must be consulted. It will also be necessary to call in an engineer who is experienced in historic structures.

If the cracks are full of dirt they may be old ones; pronounced distortions in timber-framed buildings may have taken place long ago. Sagging floors may be due to the original reuse of beams from previous buildings, while severely eroded timbers may still be of adequate size for the job they are doing in an unused building. Cracks due to shrinkable clay subsoils may be opening and closing again with changes in climatic conditions.

Where progressive movements are thought to exist the cracks must be monitored. Glass 'tell-tales' are no longer used because it is not the movement itself that is necessarily important but its magnitude, direction, and pattern.

Sophisticated systems for monitoring buildings are available if required, but normally the monitoring is carried out, after a thorough structural assessment, by fixing tiny drilled stainless steel discs in sets of three on both sides of cracks so that vertical and horizontal

See Appendix entry 2

Fig 7 Gable and front elevation of 17 Folegate Street, Spitalfields, tied to an internal scaffold structure (photo: Anthony Richardson)

movements can be measured with a vernier gauge. Non-ferrous screws in plastic plugs are a reasonably effective substitute for the discs. The extent of leaning or bulging of vertical elements can be monitored with a plumbline using similar discs or screws to ensure that readings are always taken from the same spots.

If measurements are taken monthly it can soon be established whether movement is taking place progressively in the same direction. Monitoring can later be reduced to six-monthly intervals and after about two years a confident conclusion can be reached about the stability of the building. Hasty remedial action which is not needed for safety can cost much more than these procedures and can do more harm than good. Where monitoring is considered advisable, it should be put in hand with the temporary repairs in order to avoid delay at the time of full repair.

Advice as to experts able to carry out this work may be sought from the Structural and Civil Engineering branch of English Heritage.

The danger of actual collapse is rare, but where it is deemed to exist the structure must be restrained. Temporary restraint is carried out with support scaffolding, timber shoring, or a purpose-made supporting structure of steel. There are many pitfalls and disadvantages in the use of temporary supports and it is always worthwhile to consider first whether the structure could itself be improved at an equivalent or lower cost. A rotten wall plate may be replaced with masonry, a bulge rebuilt, some weak masonry grouted, or the cause of the impending failure corrected. In these and many other cases permanent work may be less expensive than temporary. Very limited temporary strengthening may be adequate, such as wind-bracing the roof structure or framing and bracing the window openings. Where a temporary supporting structure is used, the following points should be considered:

See Appendix entry 3

- In normal building work responsibility for the provision of scaffolding is left to the contractor. This arrangement is unsuitable for support structures; they must be designed by a reputable scaffold firm and then checked and supervised by the owner's engineer. In difficult cases the engineer should give the scaffold designer preliminary guidelines. The same principle applies to timber shoring.

- All concerned must be aware that the temporary supports are to support, but not move, the structure.

- Wherever possible support structures should be designed to tie the building together from inside (Fig 7). External shoring sometimes does more harm than good, and sometimes does nothing at all. Case study 1 shows problems with both types.

- The supports should be designed as far as possible in relation to the work that will ultimately take place. It will be an advantage if they can remain in place for the first stages of the permanent repair contract and not provide too much of an impediment to the access scaffolding and the building work.

- Foundations are an integral part of the temporary structure. Scaffold boards are generally too thin and will rot on wet ground. Base plates must be fully supported. Railway sleepers should not be used where creosote staining would be detrimental.

● Rust stains on the elevations must be avoided. Standard galvanised tube is suitable but cut ends will rust and tightening the bolts removes the galvanising. Nylon caps should be used where the tube ends are near the building and the fittings should be protected where rusting could stain the building. The wall piece must always be of timber.

● Window glass should preferably not be broken for through ties to be inserted; old glass is likely to be hand-made and valuable. It is better to open the window where appropriate and fix it to prevent further opening. Birds should always be excluded by fitting mesh or plywood.

● The scaffolders themselves must be briefed about the care of an historic building and their work must be supervised. Much damage can be done through carelessness especially when the scaffold is being dismantled; too often equipment is dropped from a height, breaking the paving on to which it lands, and supports are moved before the building is stabilised. Transferring the load from temporary to permanent support requires much care and accuracy.

● Yearly inspections and maintenance are needed to check that the support structure is still doing the job for which it was designed. Scaffolding is bound to move, owing to the multiplicity of joints; props go out of plumb, bolts rust, and components are removed. Foundations become undermined and settle. Timber shoring is liable to shrink and swell and wedges must be adjusted.

Fig 8 Support for brickwork which was pushed out by a fallen truss in the North Warehouse, Gloucester Docks; this scaffolding was hired initially for three years but remained in place from 1975 to 1985 (photo: Richard Parsons)

Fig 9 The value of the building is not reflected in the character of the notice (photo: Kent Building Preservation Trust)

Fig 10 A temporary stairway leading to otherwise inaccessible parts of Maw's Tileworks, Ironbridge (photo: A T Herbert)

- Where the future of the building is uncertain it may be worth considering buying the scaffolding: it will be uneconomic to hire it for more than two to three years (Fig 8). A reputable scaffold firm will design, supply, and erect a scheme and sell it with an agreement to dismantle and buy it back at a prearranged rate, possibly the original price less a percentage for every year it has been in use.

2.4.2 Public safety and access

The building must be made safe for inspection, including that by potential users and buyers, during its period of temporary repair.

'Keep Out' notices should be as small as is compatible with visibility. Notices should always be neat and permanent; scrawled notices on salvaged material devalue an historic building (Fig 9).

The building must be made safe for people using public rights of way and those on adjoining private land.

Railings for basements are not usually necessary except on town pavements, and here a very strong case should be put to the local authority for a grant for permanent railings, since they fulfil the needs of both public safety and townscape. A good-looking, child-proof, temporary rail on a Georgian street is almost impossible to provide.

The interior of the building should be free of unseen hazards such as rotten boards, unprotected stairwells, and missing stair treads. Holes in floors should be protected or boarded over. Rooms with no floors should be visible, with doors fixed open and bars across the door frames. The removal of debris is essential. Some buildings will need temporary stairs or secured ladders internally, and single rail handrails. Access ways to inaccessible parts of large buildings should be constructed or repaired, and protected with single handrails (Fig 10).

Exterior features which might fall on members of the public should be permanently fixed or removed and stored as has already been described (see section 2.3). Old television aerials should be removed to prevent chimney or roof damage.

2.4.3 Protection from traffic

Historic buildings in poor condition could be vulnerable to damage from traffic in the following circumstances:

- Where temporary shoring projects across the footway. In this case a temporary barrier will need to be provided in consultation with the police and the highway authority.

- Where heavy vehicles pass very close to an already weakened building and it is possible that vibrations could exacerbate existing defects. If there is a pronounced irregularity in the road the momentary vibrations can have a considerably increased effect. A wise precaution would be to ask the highway authority to correct any obvious defects.

- Where cellars with brick vaulting or stone slab roofs extend below the footway and are at risk from vehicles mounting the kerb. The height between the soffit of the cellar roof and the pavement surface above should be measured and the condition of the structure checked. Permanent repair or temporary support may be indicated. The presence of the cellars often makes a difference to the feasibility of a conversion scheme; therefore it is better to avoid filling them up at temporary repair stage. If it is essential to fill, all rubbish and timber should be removed or the blocked cellar will become a source of dry rot.

Fig 11 The possibility of direct impact from a heavy vehicle cannot be ignored (photo: The Civic Trust)

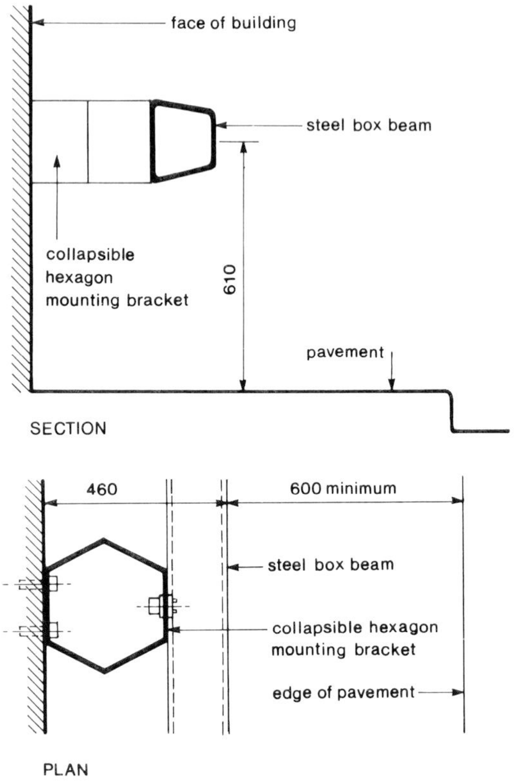

Fig 12 Traffic barrier fixed to building

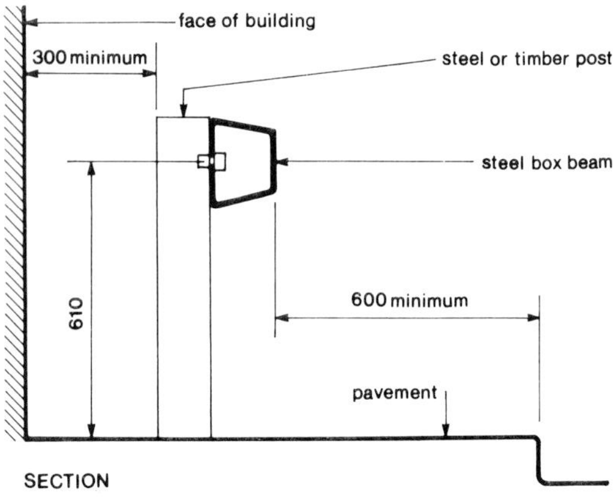

Fig 13 Free-standing traffic barrier

● Where the building is very close to the road and at risk from vehicular impact (Fig 11). A traffic barrier can be fixed directly to a building in the form of a steel box beam with collapsible hexagon mounting brackets. This will give a projection of 460mm. Every effort should be made to achieve a pavement width of not less than 1060mm, giving 600mm between the beam face and the road kerb (Fig 12). Free-standing barriers are required to be placed with a minimum clearance of 300mm between the posts and the building and a set-back from the kerb of 600mm. In this case pedestrians may have to be considered, as well as problems connected with post foundations in the footway (Fig 13). The correct design and installation of the barrier with entry and terminal points should be carried out in conjunction with the highway authority.

2.5 Security

2.5.1 Assessing security

An empty building is vulnerable to intruders, vandals, and thieves. The best protection is to find a temporary user, as will be discussed in chapter 3. Vacancy can generally be foreseen and security should be considered as a matter of urgency before the building becomes empty. Assess the security of the building by considering the following three factors:

- The degree of risk. This varies according to the neighbourhood and is higher in larger communities and inner city areas than in smaller communities, but rises again in certain isolated situations.

- The exact nature of the items to be protected. These might be the lead on the roof, the window glass, the enrichments, the floorboards, the wall surfaces, or fixtures such as fireplaces, cupboards, panelling, and staircases.

- The vulnerability of the building. Contributory factors include local isolation, ill-lit surroundings, concealed entrances, low roofs, shrubberies, outbuildings, and the degree of disrepair.

2.5.2 Assistance with security

If a temporary user cannot be found, a caretaker is needed. He or she may be employed to live in and look after the building, or may work there for an hour a week, or at the very least be a keyholder with a telephone. In the latter case someone whose daily activities involve passing the building will be more effective.

Assistance and advice on security can then be obtained as follows:

- Supervision by the police. The amount of supervision which the police can give to an empty building varies according to the circumstances; if they are not aware of the problem they will certainly do nothing. The valuable nature of the building should be explained to the local police who may be able to include it on a beat; the supervision can be made easier by attention to the surroundings and by giving them the telephone number of the keyholder. It is worth reporting every act of vandalism simply and accurately to the police in writing; they will otherwise have no means of assessing the problem.

- Advice from the police. To obtain the best advice contact the force crime prevention officer at the force headquarters. He will probably delegate a divisional crime prevention officer to discuss physical protection on the site.

- Assistance from the local authority. Many boroughs have their own security officer and he may be able to include the building on an already established inspection list or nightly tour by a security guard.

- Assistance from neighbours. Contact the adjoining owners and those who overlook the site, explain the value of the building, and ask them to cooperate unofficially. If they have a caretaker or an alarm, official connections could be considered.

See Appendix entry 4

- Support from the community. Get in touch with the local amenity society; some of their members may pass the building each day and be prepared to report any damage immediately. They may be keen to do more than this in helping to care for a local building.

2.5.3 Deterring vandals

If the external appearance of the building can be maintained, vandalism may never occur, but at any stage of deterioration the following measures are worthwhile and inexpensive; they should be put in hand immediately, whenever the circumstances are applicable:

- Tidy up the surroundings, remove rubbish, and make the building look cared for.

- Prune shrubs, clip hedges, and remove any undergrowth or unwanted plants that conceal the entrances.

- Remove rubble that can be picked up and thrown (Fig 14).

- Put cheap net curtains in the windows to give a semblance of occupation to the casual passer-by and to conceal the interior.

- Fit locks to all accessible windows.

Fig 14 A good supply of missiles left ready at the back of listed Southfields Square, Bradford, in 1982

- Reglaze a broken window immediately.

- Remove graffiti immediately (see section 2.5.7).

- Consider extra external lighting, taking advice on security wiring and fittings, and using low or high pressure sodium lamps for long life and economy.

2.5.4 Physical protection

Fig 15 The Roundhouse Chapel, Manchester, was very strongly protected in 1978 while waiting for a new use, but vandals penetrated the structure itself, finding the old masonry weaker than the new (photo: The North West Civic Trust)

Look at the building from all sides and the roof, bearing in mind that a slim person or a child can get through a hole only 230×230mm (9″×9″) or even 255×200mm (10″×8″). Do not forget to consider skylights, cellar flaps, fuel shutes, and upper floor windows accessible from lower roofs.

The cost of protection must be considered in relation to the financial and historic value of the interior. It may be decided not to spend money on protecting outbuildings or certain parts of the building itself.

Temporary protection should not be much stronger than the surrounding fabric. It is not possible to exclude a determined intruder and it is better for the temporary protection to be destroyed than the fabric itself (Fig 15).

The measures described below are minimum measures for unoccupied historic buildings and are designed to deter the opportunist intruder.

A External doors

Fig 16 Temporary internal frame for a door which is not needed for access

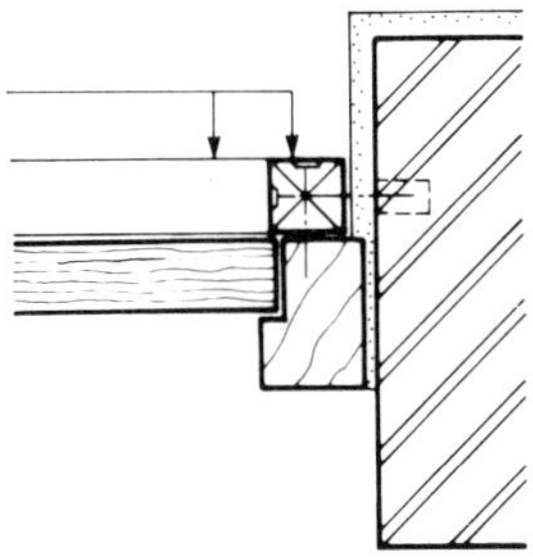

All external doors, except those needed for access, should be fixed shut. Glazed doors, those with panels less than 22mm thick, and hollow flush doors should be protected with 12mm ply screwed to the inside. Vertically boarded doors do not give security because the boards can be removed; they need external protection with 12mm exterior (WBP) ply. If the door frame moves, strap it to the wall internally with three steel straps. Strong bolts top and bottom, with the existing door furniture centrally, should be adequate; if the bolt staples are weak, cover them with steel straps screwed twice above and below. If the door opens outwards the hinge side may be secured with dog bolts. In the case of these unused doors an alternative to strengthening the frame and fixings is to put softwood framing inside, screwed to plugs in the wall and to the frame and door (Fig 16).

B Access door

Choose an external door in a conspicuous and well-lit position for access. The door and frame need checking and protection as in A above, but instead of bolts, provide two locks reasonably spaced on the door. This will probably be the existing medium to high position and one new one at 'booting in' level. Expensive locks are unnecessary; a single throw, five lever, British Standard (kite-marked) mortice dead lock is adequate; it should have a boxed striking plate and, being a permanent item, must be carefully fixed so as not to damage the door. For doors less than 44mm thick, a rim lock is stronger than a mortice lock, but the striking plate must be side-fixed. To test an existing lock, see that the bolt fits tight in the case; there should be no vertical or horizontal movement, whether the bolt is projecting or withdrawn; the throw must not be less than 12mm providing the gap does not exceed 3mm; two lever locks are unsuitable.

The access door should never be blocked up in such a way as to prevent easy inspection of the inside of the building. Where the above measures have failed, a proprietary anti-vandal door screen can be used; it is fixed by heavy adjustable jacks and has an access wicket released only by security magnets. These screens are expensive but can be adapted for repeated use.

See Appendix entry 5

C Internal doors

Internal doors should be kept shut to shield inside views from windows but they should not be locked; once inside, an intruder will damage locked doors and door casings by breaking them down.

D Windows

Deterrent measures have already been discussed (see section 2.5.3). Where these have failed and glazing cannot be maintained, protection

Fig 17 Miscellaneous blocking materials downgrade an empty church in Bedford

Fig 18 Boarding which can be levered off is ineffective; inadequate traffic protection has resulted in damage from high-sided vehicles (photo: Ann Bridger)

Fig 19 Temporary protection for an unglazed window

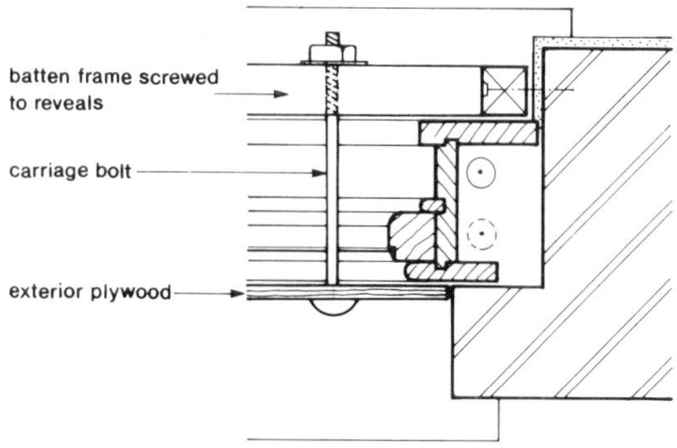

will be needed. Permanent work should be considered where the circumstances are such that it will ultimately be needed. This may involve grilles, bars, security glazing, and special fastenings. Temporary protection of windows is always difficult and not altogether desirable; it draws attention to the plight of the building and is frequently either ineffective or else blocks ventilation and causes damage to the windows or the reveals. Temporary methods may nevertheless be adopted to reduce costs, but miscellaneous types of blocking materials, unrendered masonry units, old doors, corrugated iron, and scrap materials should never be used (Fig 17).

Ventilation of an empty building is of the utmost importance and must be considered in conjunction with window protection; this will be discussed in section 2.6.4. With this in mind, one or other of the following temporary methods could be employed:

- Where the glass is already broken use 18 or 20mm exterior quality plywood fixed externally but cut to fit inside the reveals and set back from the outside face of the building. The aim is to allow no cracks which would admit implements to lever the plywood off (Fig 18). Bolt the ply with 'cup square' carriage bolts and nuts to battens fixed internally. Paint or stain the plywood (Figs 19 and 20).

- Where the glazed windows are intact and the external reveals are at least 140mm deep (or 115mm for small windows), 100mm (or 75mm) blockwork can be used and rendered over. The face of the

Fig 20 Neat and effective protection which could be painted or stained

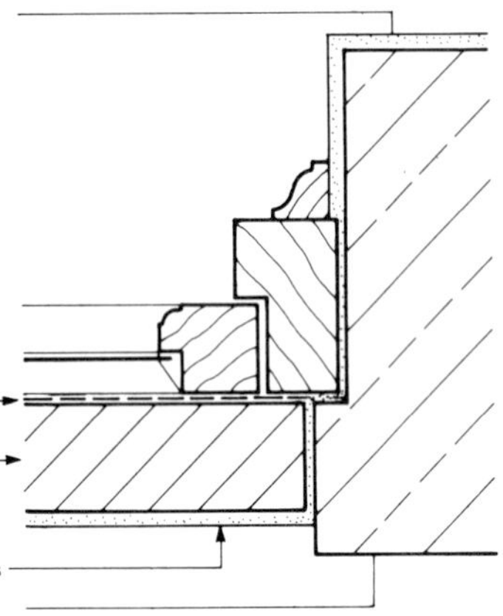

Fig 21 Temporary blocking for intact window

rendering must be set back from the wall face; the strength of the mortar and the rendering must not be greater than 1:2:9 (cement:lime:sand); strong cement mortar will damage the reveals and arrises of the permanent structure at the time of removal. All masonry construction can of course be easily removed before the mortar has achieved its full strength. If this is a probability it will be necessary to guard the building (Fig 21).

Fig 22 Single skin blockwork has been penetrated by vandals whilst unprotected windows and skylights admit birds and rain; Southfields Square, Bradford, in 1982

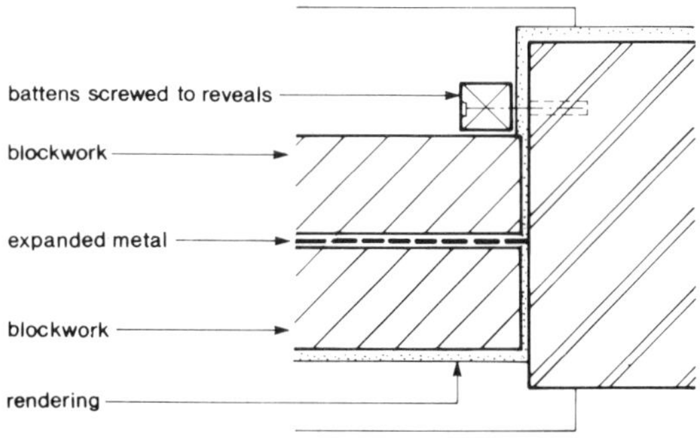

Fig 23 Extreme protection where joinery has not survived

See Appendix entry 6

See Appendix entry 7

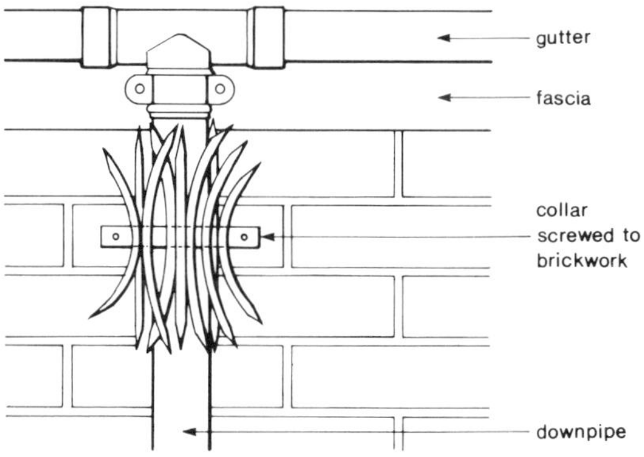

Fig 24 Spiked collar on rainwater pipe to deter climbing

See Appendix entry 8

● Windows should not be removed, but where this has already been done, blockwork or plywood should be set well back. Where extra strength is required expanded metal can be fixed behind the blockwork to the inner surface of the wall, or it can be incorporated in a sandwich construction; timber battens screwed to plugs in reveals can restrain the whole panel on the inside (Figs 22 and 23).

E Roofs

Everything possible must be done to make the roofs inaccessible. Once on the roof an intruder can remove tiles and get in, steal the lead, get through a skylight, or at the very least damage the roof coverings.

Anti-climb paint looks unpleasant and attracts dirt but it may be the only effective way to prevent the climbing of rainwater pipes; it should be applied for a height of 1m with the lowest part 2.4m from the ground. Spiked collars can be fixed to pipes just below the gutter but should not be placed near window sills where they could provide a foothold (Fig 24). Remove all redundant or faulty waste pipes and soil pipes, and also other aids to climbing such as branches, boxes, and unwanted sheds.

Glass should be removed from accessible skylights and the frame covered with exterior quality ply and roofing felt, and strongly secured from within.

If the roof cannot be made reasonably inaccessible and there is a known threat to the lead, or if thefts of lead have actually started, it may be necessary to remove it all and substitute, for example, a tiled ridge with zinc, nuralite, or temporary felt flashings.

2.5.5 Fire precautions

A high proportion of fires are started deliberately. Empty buildings are much more vulnerable to arson than those which are occupied. Therefore, when considering an empty historic building, the fire risk should not be ignored.

The advice of the county fire prevention officer should be sought. He will have useful recommendations to make in the light of his experience of fires in similar situations and will recommend an appropriate level of fire fighting equipment.

The measures already discussed to deter and exclude vandals apply just as much to fire raisers. Rubbish and any inflammable materials should be cleared from outside and inside the building. Cellars, cupboards, roof spaces, and attics are often packed with rubbish.

A common method of deliberate ignition is through the letter box. This could therefore be given a firmly screwed-on cover on the inside, or else a closed metal letter container. For the same reason gaps under external doors could be sealed.

Electricity and gas supplies should be cut off unless they are vitally necessary. If supplies must be maintained see that they are tested and that recommended remedial measures are taken.

Fires can be started accidentally by the builders or volunteers who are cleaning up the building and putting the repairs in hand. Fires should never be lit inside an historic building; fireplaces, hearths, and flues are frequently defective and a smouldering fire may be started in floor timbers. Rubbish should always be burned outside and well away from the building. No smoking or blow lamps should be allowed.

A mess room for contractors, volunteers, or security personnel can be a fire hazard and if possible should be away from the building. If this is not possible, choose the room with the best fire resistance and means of escape. Insist on good housekeeping, meticulous daily rubbish disposal, and safe tea-making, water heating, room heating, and fuel storage. Provide a self-contained, battery-operated smoke detector and a fire extinguisher.

In the case of important buildings the fire service may be prepared to formulate an emergency plan. This would refer to access, water supply, constructional hazards, and all possible measures to protect valuable features of the building from water damage.

2.5.6 Intruder alarms

A complete protection system will usually be inappropriate for an empty building. The protection of a single room or self-contained section of a building could however be justified for the sake of its decoration, plasterwork, fire surrounds, joinery, or contents. This can be achieved by a variety of trigger devices such as volumetric detection by infrared, ultrasonic, or microwave detectors, contact points on mats or doors, or vibrator contacts set off by a hammer and chisel on the masonry. This equipment can be used to actuate a piercing noise in the room, a sounder outside, a signal to the police station (wired by British Telecom), or a floodlight. The least expensive is a self-contained device including battery, volumetric protection, and sounder. It would have be placed out of reach, preferably behind a strongly fixed grille.

Alarm protection is liable to be ineffective in a dilapidated or poorly constructed building. The trigger device can often be affected by wind, water, fumes, birds, cats, or excessive exposure. The installation must be inspected every three to four months and the batteries must be trickle charged or an electricity supply maintained (which can itself be cut off). Most important of all, an alarm system cannot be considered unless there is a local keyholding service the cost of which can be justified by the valuable nature of the interior.

The insurers, and possibly the fire prevention officer, may advise that an alarm system is the only valid protection against deliberate ignition. The police may take a different view and the most helpful procedure may be to invite the crime and fire prevention officers to attend a meeting together.

If, having considered these factors, an alarm system is thought to be appropriate, the National Supervisory Council for Intruder Alarms can give the names of approved installers.

See Appendix entry 9

2.5.7 Graffiti

Graffiti attract more graffiti and, if the affected wall surface is accessible, the only cure is to clean it repeatedly before other vandals can see it. This often requires extreme determination and persistence.

If a porous surface has been defaced, immediate cleaning will be much more effective than waiting: hours matter; the same day is much better than the next day, and the day after is much better than waiting for a week. Use a proprietary gel or else nitromors, methylated spirit, or cellulose thinners depending on the type of paint to be removed. Do not use caustic soda. The pigment in the graffiti is very easily driven further into a soft stone or brick surface and in these cases a poultice covered with a plastic sheet can be used to draw it out. If a residue remains which cannot be removed, it can sometimes be concealed by stippling very lightly with paint to match the background.

To protect a limited area of walling from being penetrated by paint and to make removal relatively easy, special barrier treatments are available. The most successful are those which line the pores of the masonry with a water-repellent coating and do not trap moisture behind the treated surface. These materials are unsuitable for decaying surfaces and the only answer here may be to wait for permanent repair by replacement or consolidation.

See Appendix entry 10

2.6 Excluding water

2.6.1 Roofs

Before repairing the roof, attend to any features at a higher level. Remove loose chimney pots to store, repair unsafe stacks, exclude birds, remove TV aerials, leave flues open for ventilation.

Inspect the roof space up to all edges and corners to see where timbers are damp; inspect in a heavy rainstorm to observe leaks; check ceilings for signs of damp, especially below parapet and valley gutters.

A Slate and tile

Provide a new permanent roof or carry our permanent repairs whenever possible. Failing that, carry out patch repairs to the existing roof in matching second-hand materials. This will achieve a better interim appearance and give some security against intruders.

If neither of these measures is possible, a temporary covering will have to be considered. Remove the remaining slates or tiles and stack them for later reuse. Repair the roof timbers with pressure-treated timber and provide a covering which may eventually be used as the underslating felt. Normal underslating felts are only intended to be exposed for a month or so; they contain inadequate bitumen for prolonged exposure. Translucent polythene is sometimes thought to be an advantage in order to provide natural light below. For this material to last longer than about six months it must contain an ultraviolet inhibitor ('UVI grade') and unfortunately this is not normally incorporated in material of suitable thickness. Therefore, if polythene is chosen, it should be black. For an exposed roofing application a suitable thickness is 300 or 375 micrometres which is readily available (1 micrometre = .001mm). A familiar material is 1200 gauge damp proof membrane (coloured blue for site identification); this is 300 micrometres thick but as it has no UVI it is not suitable for exposed roofing. A bituminous material would also be suitable but must contain enough bitumen not to be leached out by rain and must have very good resistance to wind tearing. A polyester-based felt, fairly light in weight but very difficult to tear, could be employed.

See Appendix entry 11

Whichever alternative is used for a temporary roof covering, all the joints should be lapped by 150mm and taped against wind lift with a wide tape as recommended by the makers of the sheet (black in the case of the polythene). The sheeting or felt must be taken well into the gutter and could be taped into it with Sylglas standard mastic tape. The felt or sheeting should be laid fairly tight (but not stretched) and fixed down with treated vertical battens nailed through the sheeting to the top of each rafter.

See Appendix entry 12

Temporary repair with bitumenised fabric over slates is very seldom applicable, as the slates can never be reused in the future. Proprietary measures for securing slates from below when the nails have failed must also be scrutinised critically; if the fixing material cannot be removed, it will again prevent the reuse of the sound slates.

B Lead

A defective lead roof must be permanently repaired according to the best practice, or else removed, the best price being obtained for the lead. Minor defects can be temporarily treated as described in section 2.6.2 for lead gutters. Bituminous strips and compounds should never be used. Self-adhesive strips are pointless when placed over joints which are there to allow the lead to move, but they can be useful for local defects.

C Asphalt

Temporary repairs to asphalt roofs can be carried out with one of the many sets of proprietary repairing products which are now available. A crack needs to be scraped clean, filled with bituminous mastic, covered with a well-bedded reinforcing strip of canvas, and painted over with waterproofing compound. Choose a system incorporating these components and follow the instructions exactly. Liquid coatings for roof repair, simply painted on in two coats, will be ineffective except for filling hair cracks. In sunny positions finish the surface with solar reflective paint.

See Appendix entry 13

D Felt

A felt roof, although itself a temporary finish for an historic building, may still need temporary repair. 'Torch on' roofings are now claimed to be the most effective repair materials as well as being the easiest to apply. The material is very tough and incorporates its own adhesive which is activated by the use of a propane torch. Before a patch repair is made, the area has to be cleaned and dried, and fire precautions taken.

See Appendix entry 14

E Tarpaulins

These are a very short-term emergency measure accompanied by obvious difficulties in tying down, drainage, and linking with other coverings, abutments, and flashings. A 'belly' in the tarpaulin frequently fills with water and empties into the building. However, they provide some protection immediately while proper measures are considered.

F *Flashings*

The repair of flashings is vital, especially where tall abutments on an exposed face collect large quantities of rain which runs down on to a roof below. Proprietary flashing strips are of very limited value here because the water will get behind them. A 40mm chase with a temporary flashing of mineral-surfaced felt will be more effective. The effective use of self-adhesive flashing strips, where they are applicable, depends upon the preparation of the background to which they are to be stuck; follow the instructions, always use the correct primer, and do not use them on friable surfaces.

2.6.2 Rainwater systems

Fig 25 Complete lack of protection at eaves level in 1981 resulted in disastrous erosion of the stonework at Barlborough Old Hall (photo: Bob Hawkins)

Trace the rainwater routes from all exposed surfaces to their ultimate disposal at ground level (Fig 25) and inspect the building during a heavy rainstorm. Clean the rainwater goods and the valley and parapet gutters and test the efficiency of below ground gulleys and drains. Where roof lines are complicated, the existing rainwater system may be badly designed; gutters may be virtually inaccessible and downpipes may be discharging in unsuitable places. It is worth considering temporary improvements to make the system easier to observe and to keep clear of leaves. For example, if a downpipe from a high level gutter discharges on to a lower roof it is possible to omit the gutter altogether and throw the water clear of the wall by the insertion of sheet zinc below the roof coverings (Fig 26).

See Appendix entry 15

Bandage cracked downpipes and sockets with standard mastic tape. Line defective cast iron gutters with the same material. Faults and cracks are revealed by water stains and growths on the masonry. Replace all lengths where repair is not possible; when PVC has to be used make sure to obtain it in black and beware of using it in situations which are vulnerable to damage and vandalism. Install overflow shutes to the ends of parapet gutters.

Repairs to lead valley and parapet gutters will often be needed. Lead tends to split when the pieces are too large or when movement of each piece is prevented by incorrect fixings. A temporary repair in a valley gutter is achieved by cutting the lead, thus allowing it to move, and inserting another section lapping below the upper and above the lower piece. Depending on the fall and exposure this could be a permanent repair. In other situations temporary repairs to last from one to two years can be made with proprietary flashing tapes provided that they are made of adhesive rather than bituminous materials. It is essential to clean thoroughly, lightly wire brush, and dry the lead before applying the adhesive strip. This method simplifies regular inspection; it is possible to see what has been done and to peel off the tape when permanent repair is undertaken. Bituminous materials do not last when applied to lead; they conceal subsequent defects and reduce the salvage value of the metal. If the lead is badly damaged, and especially if theft is a possibility, it may be best to

Fig 26 The Church House at Widecombe-in-the-Moor shows that no gutter at high level can sometimes be better than one that is inaccessible, even in a permanent situation

remove and sell it, and use the proceeds to employ a specialist firm to install temporary felt gutters. This involves removing the lowest three rows of slating or tiling nearest to the gutter, laying the felt, and replacing the slates or tiles. If this position is not visible, nibbed concrete tiles can be used, which are more easily lifted later when the permanent gutter lining is fixed. The use of the substitutes in a concealed position allows original slates or tiles to be removed and put aside for patch repairs.

At ground level, pay special attention to gulleys and gratings in enclosed areas where blockages would cause the water level to rise against the building. This is doubly important in the case of timber-framed buildings with timber sole plates. Consider putting leaf guards over gulleys. Rod drains if necessary or arrange temporary disposal channels. Avoid open trenches at the base of walls, as damage can be done to shallow footings and supporting subsoil can be exposed to frost.

Arrange for regular inspection and cleaning of all rainwater systems, exercising even more vigilance that would be needed for a fully repaired building.

2.6.3 Rising damp

Damp proof courses became general practice after the 1875 and 1891 Public Health Acts. Always look for a damp proof course even if the building is older. It is usually in a mortar course either above or below the level of the ventilation grilles and, if present, is probably effective although often 'bridged'. It is seldom advisable or necessary to consider a new damp proof course, either inserted or injected, at emergency repair stage. If this is ultimately needed, it should be preceded by full preparations made in conjunction with any replanning of the building.

Where there are signs of rising damp, the following simple measures should be considered wherever they are applicable:

- Remove earth or fuel piled against the external walls above the bearing level of the joists or wall plates, or above a solid floor level.

- Remove external rendering below the dpc line.

- Remove external sand and cement plinths (usually added erroneously to prevent water penetration).

- Remove rubbish from any spaces below the ground floor boards.

- Clear ventilators and add others so that cross ventilation below the ground floor and around all the joists is possible.

- Drain or pump flooded cellars, opening up flues if possible to promote drying.

- Lift floor boards next to wet walls, remove the nails, and leave the boards upside down beside the slot from which they have been removed.

2.6.4 Drying out and ventilation

After the ingress of moisture has been prevented and rising damp minimised, the building must be dried out and kept dry and ventilated. The aim is to reduce the moisture content of the timber to below 22% so that it cannot sustain the growth of fungi.

There is no rule of thumb about areas of permanent ventilation; it depends upon the amount of moisture present and the size of the building. The principle is to remove unwanted wet features, expose all other wet features, and promote a 'stack' ventilation system rising through the building with the moist air being removed by cross ventilation at the top.

Cross ventilation of roof spaces is desirable at temporary and permanent stages. Temporary roof coverings of impervious material with taped joints will make the situation more acute. A rule of thumb for adequate ventilation of normal domestic spans is the equivalent of a 25mm continuous slot on opposing sides of the roof.

See Appendix entry 16

See Appendix entry 17

Where there are opposing gable walls, cross ventilation can be provided by plastic ventilators which fit unobtrusively into brick perpends, or suitable masonry joints can be left open. Rendered walls may have to be drilled and the holes lined with plastic piping. Where there are no suitable gables, ventilation can sometimes be provided behind the gutter. This can be arranged through the soffit or by means of a continuous slot behind the fascia. Where a roof slope is concealed, proprietary ventilators can be inserted into the tilework. Where flues are no longer connected to fireplaces, a half-brick can be removed to connect with the roof space. Ventilation holes that could admit birds should be covered internally with 25mm mesh. 25mm is too small an aperture for any bird, but 28mm is large enough for a blue tit and 32mm will admit a sparrow.

Ceiling traps must be provided for access to roof spaces and, if ample ventilation at roof level is assured, the open traps will promote ventilation of the rooms below. On the other hand, in occupied or heated buildings, especially if the ceiling is insulated, the traps must be shut to prevent moist air rising to the roof space and condensing on the underside of the roof coverings.

The following additional measures should be considered wherever they are applicable:

- Form new ventilation openings near or below ground floor level.

- Open up all the fireplaces, sweep the flues, and clear the hearths. Put wire netting to exclude birds at the chimney tops if necessary, but never seal the flues.

See Appendix entry 18

- Remove floor coverings and lift floor boards next to outside walls as for rising damp (see section 2.6.3) and remove wet pugging and rubbish from between the joists.

- Very carefully remove panelling and skirtings where walls are wet behind and store them in an unheated ventilated room. It may sometimes be possible to remove the panels only, leaving the frames in place.

- Open up all wet localities such as stud partitions, cupboards, soffits of stairs, sash window boxes, and all similar places where plaster is wet and timber is concealed behind.

- Remove all rubbish and wet plaster from the building.

- Break contact between timber and wet masonry. This may mean removing bricks from around and over damp ends of joists and inserting slate below the bearing. It may mean temporary support and the sawing off of ends which are thoroughly rotten.

Arrangements for ventilation frequently conflict with security arrangements and fire precautions, and a compromise will have to be reached. Ventilation openings may have to be protected internally with expanded steel mesh; internal doors may have to be propped ajar; on the upper floors sash windows can be fitted with security stops enabling them to be left with a 100mm opening. Blocked windows may have to incorporate ventilation grilles.

2.6.5 Cocooning

The expression is used to signify wrapping up a building to give it complete protection from the weather. Protection takes the form of corrugated iron, corrugated translucent sheeting, or reinforced PVC sheeting over a framework of scaffolding.

Because of its great expense, its vulnerability to wind and vandals, and its unfortunate appearance, a cocoon of this nature is rarely used.

However, one application is where it not only protects a valuable building in a swiftly deteriorating condition, but also protects the workforce and improves conditions for permanent repair. Unless there is an immediate prospect of a repair contract, it is difficult to imagine a situation where a cocoon would be desirable or financially justifiable. On the other hand, it could pay for itself before and during a building contract by speeding up the work in adverse weather conditions, by protecting all parts of the building from further damage, and by enabling intricate and delicate work to be carried out to a higher standard.

Erecting the scaffolding and the sheeting is a specialist job and should be carefully coordinated to suit the exact building work to be undertaken and the type of sheeting chosen. The factors to be considered are the anticipated contract period, the degree of exposure, the amount of daylight needed, the number and size of access points for workers and materials, and the need for a flame retardant material. The spacing of supports and the tying or fixing of the sheeting are of the utmost importance. Loose corrugated iron is very dangerous to persons and buildings. Torn sheeting is a useless aggravation. Numerous grades of material are available with well-designed fixing methods; they can be obtained by using experienced firms, whose advice should be sought.

See Appendix entry 19

2.6.6 Screening of openings

Screening of openings, windows, or whole walls, where light is needed inside, can be carried out with reinforced polythene (Fig 27).

Fig 27 Temporary screening to a gable wall of the Liberal Club, Newcastle upon Tyne, in 1982; the upper part was translucent to facilitate internal repairs, the lower part was solid to deter intruders (photo: City Engineer, Newcastle upon Tyne)

This should have an ultraviolet inhibitor as for roofs, unless the opening is not exposed to sun. Where intruders are not a problem, nylon or polyester mesh reinforcement would be suitable. This material should be nailed to softwood studs at 600mm centres with fixing laths over the polythene. If the screen is to provide some security it should be wire reinforced; chicken wire or weld mesh can be obtained sandwiched between two layers of light gauge UVI polythene and this can be fixed with staples to the inside of the framing. It is easy to puncture the polythene, but it will not tear beyond the mesh and can be mended with polypropylene tape. It can give a degree of security to upper windows with some holes intentionally cut for ventilation.

2.6.7 Water supplies

In empty buildings disconnect the water supply and drain down all tanks and pipes. Consult the fire service if there are any doubts about water for fire fighting. In partly occupied buildings, or where the supply must be maintained, there may be a difficult problem of frost protection for pipes passing through unoccupied areas. Pipe lagging sections which are sold for domestic heating installations are inadequate for protection against frost. Pipes and tanks should be sheltered from cold winds and protected to the water authorities' standards. However, no amount of protection will prevent static water from eventually freezing in a prolonged period of hard frost; in these conditions the occupier must be aware of the need to draw off water late at night and early in the morning. The system must be drained when the building is temporarily empty and there is any risk of frost. Temporary repairs may involve measures to facilitate this.

See Appendix entry 20

2.7 Organisms

2.7.1 Fungi

Methods for controlling all wood-rotting fungi are similar and can be considered in three successive categories as follows:

A *Primary measures*

These are concerned with drying out the building and thus the wet wood which is the food source of the fungi. The overwhelming importance of these primary measures has been described in section 2.6 above, including the break to be made between timber and wet masonry. Once the moisture content of the timber is below 22% the fungi will cease their activity and gradually die. In the case of dry rot, this will take some time, perhaps several years in an unheated building. Therefore the second category of measures is needed.

B *Containment measures*

Infected wood is removed and temporary support provided as required. Residual living fungus is then prevented from spreading from the walls; this is done by brush application of a dry rot killer for masonry. After the plaster has been removed and the masonry vigorously brushed with a stiff brush, two coats are applied and worked well into cracks. Attempts to irrigate the walls are expensive and set back the much more desirable process of drying out; in any case saturation is probably impossible to achieve.

C *Protective measures*

These measures are to protect the wood itself in the event of the other measures failing. Chemicals brushed into timber *in situ* are virtually useless in killing fungi, but they can protect valuable timbers which have not yet been attacked. Bodied mayonnaise trowelled on to timber to give a deeper penetration can be more effective but must be done with skill and can bleed into plaster. Any new timber introduced into the building is vulnerable and must be pressure-treated in advance.

The use of wood preservation firms is usually inappropriate at emergency repair stage. These firms are normally organised to provide a package deal of total treatment (however unnecessary) and a 30-year guarantee. They carry out the work at maximum speed and do not necessarily have the skills for the careful treatment of an historic building.

2.7.2 Woodboring insects

See Appendix entry 21

Where there is evidence of attack by woodboring insects the species should be identified and the dangers assessed according to procedures which are well documented elsewhere.

The two following types are those which most commonly cause concern in historic buildings needing emergency repairs:

A *Furniture beetle*

Degradation by this beetle is very slow except in modern softwoods. In old timbers, ten years would make very little structural difference as the timber becomes less nutritious with age. Only sapwood is attacked. Old timbers sometimes have an extra span capacity due to over design. For all these reasons, chemical treatment will hardly ever be appropriate at emergency repair stage. In most cases remove friable timber and check the remaining timber size, but when valuable moulded or carved work has been attacked obtain specialist advice. All newly introduced timber must be pressure-treated.

B *Deathwatch beetle*

The larvae of this beetle form cavities inside large hardwood sections; they are scarcely affected by spray- or brush-applied chemicals. The only treatment is to reduce the colony gradually by killing the emerging beetles every year between April and June. This treatment could be begun during an emergency repair period. It is most cheaply carried out by the annual use of smoke canisters, using chemicals

See Appendix entry 22

which are not harmful to bats.

Where deathwatch beetle is present structural tests must be made, especially at beam bearings. Degradation is very slow indeed and old hardwood sections are strong, but the point of failure may just have been reached, and temporary supports could be needed. If deathwatch beetle is present in small sections, the situation may be more serious.

2.7.3 Birds

Pigeons are extraordinarily persistent in their efforts to get into a roof space and, once they are inside, their droppings will harbour damp and insects. They will even work away at a loose tile to make a small aperture. This possibility must be guarded against; ventilation openings and other apertures which are not protected for security should be covered with plastic square mesh netting, mounted on battens attached to the inside of the wall with non-ferrous fixings. After sweeping the chimneys put wire mesh or ventilated caps into the tops of chimney pots.

See Appendix entry 23

2.7.4 Harmful growths

All creepers which obscure windows, doors, and ventilators, block gutters, or threaten to penetrate tile hangings or cover roof surfaces

Fig 28 Plants flourishing in weak mortar joints with an ample water supply from broken gutters

Fig 29 Sloping surfaces harbour seeds in brick joints leading to a risk of disintegration from strongly growing plant roots

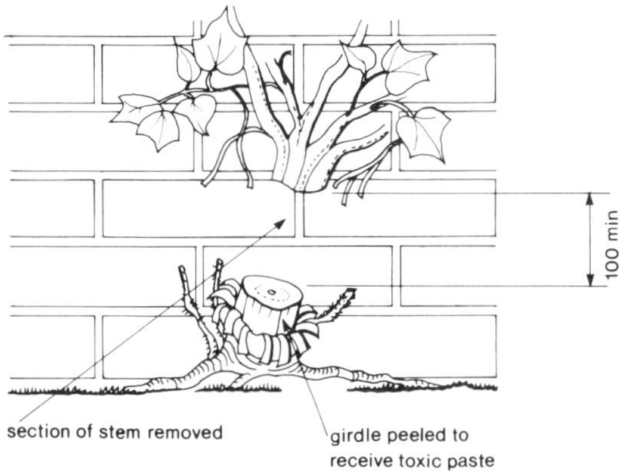

Fig 30 Killing ivy (based on *Practical building conservation*, Vol 1, by J and N Ashurst)

Fig 31 Seventeenth-century plasterwork at Barlborough Old Hall threatened by damp penetration from rubbish blocking the flue behind it (photo: Bob Hawkins)

should be cut back (Figs 28 and 29). Buddleias and antirrhinum should be carefully removed from cracks.

Ivy is positively destructive, seeking out all cracks and weaknesses and finally making the wall porous and unstable. Ivy should therefore be killed as part of the emergency repairs and be allowed to die gradually during the waiting period. It should never be pulled off while alive, and even when dead must be carefully removed while remedial work to the masonry joints is being carried out. To kill the ivy, cut a 100mm section out of the parent stem near the ground. Frill out the cut stem and treat with a paste made of ammonium sulphamate crystals (Fig 30).

Brambles growing around a neglected building may have to be killed with brushwood killer, applied during the growing season. Do not splash this product on the masonry as it will stain.

Algal slimes and moulds tend to keep the building damp. Lichens are harmless in themselves although they may eventually assist in the establishment of other plants. The treatment of these types of growth should not be hastily undertaken as an emergency repair, but should wait for careful consideration at the time of full repair.

2.8 Special features

2.8.1 External enrichments

Where stone walls are flaking it is better to remove the flakes than

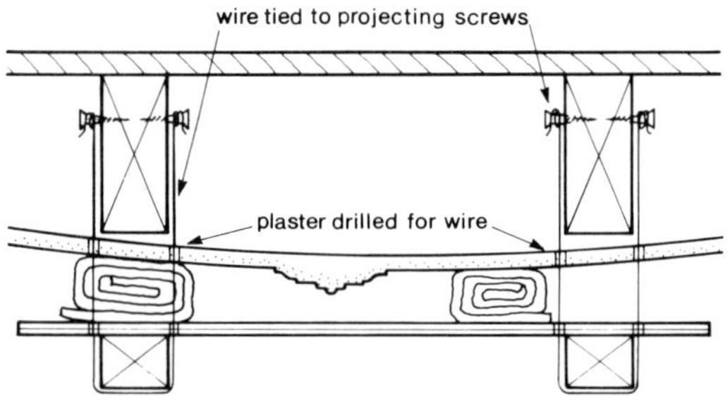

Fig 32 Temporary ceiling support with felt rolls, ply panels, bearers, and wire slings (based on *Practical building conservation*, Vol 2, by J and N Ashurst)

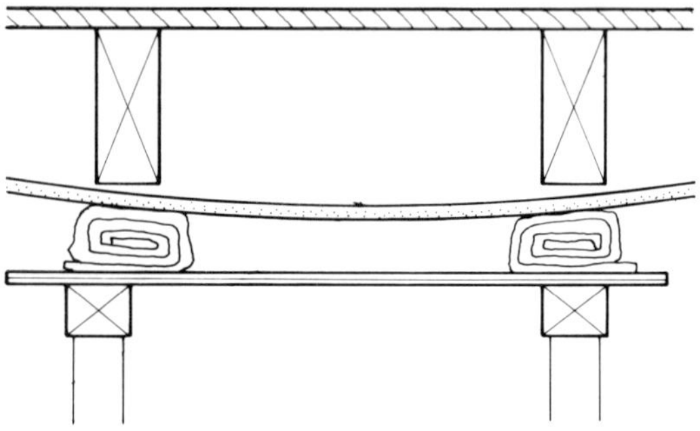

Fig 33 Temporary ceiling support with felt roll ply panels, bearers, and props (based on *Practical building conservation*, Vol 2, by J and N Ashurst)

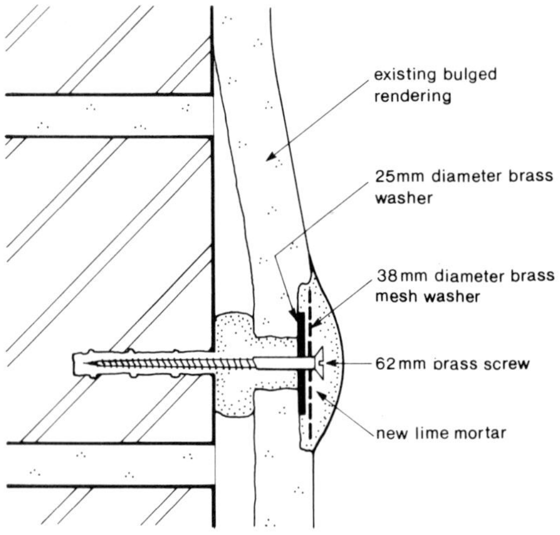

Fig 34 Rendering bulge temporarily secured

to leave loose fragments which trap water behind the face.

Where moulding or enrichments are loose and can be taken off, removal and storage will be the safest way to ensure ultimate repair. Where the fragments are too damaged for reuse they may still be wanted to crush into an aggregate for mortar repair. Large upstanding features, crumbling but suitable for ultimate repair, can sometimes be removed to temporary shelter. Such items are urns, parapet figures, pinnacles, balusters, or free-standing sculpture. If removal would be disproportionately expensive or would endanger the object, they can be boxed in position. Use treated timber and exterior quality plywood covered with roofing felt to make the box waterproof. Insulating slabs may possibly reduce the number of freeze and thaw cycles.

For enrichments attached to the facade boxing is also a possibility, but in this case the insulation should be omitted and the box ventilated. The framework should be screwed to the wall with brass screws and a proper roof and flashing provided.

Where boxing is undesirable or unnecessary, it is still essential to prevent the ingress of moisture to the back through unrepaired masonry. Holes and joints can be temporarily filled with very weak mortar. For better protection a miniature roof or temporary flashing can be made of zinc or felt, secured at the top with exposed timber battens nailed into the joints with non-ferrous nails. Proprietary self-adhesive flashings may occasionally be suitable on a smooth non-friable background, but felt and battens will last longer.

Where valuable carvings are crumbling it is necessary to record and probably to protect them. Temporary repairs are inappropriate and a sculpture conservator should be consulted.

2.8.2 Plasterwork and rendering

Thoroughly remove loose internal plasterwork, but not more than is necessary; the decision about the extent of new work should be left to the time of full repair (Fig 31). Record and store all mouldings and enrichments (see section 2.3).

Ornamental plaster ceilings will need to be temporarily supported if cracks are wide or continuous or if one edge of the crack is lower than the other. Ignore fine wandering cracks. Support the ceiling with plywood panels separated from the plaster by pads or rolls of underfelt or other soft material. Support the plywood with beams and props from the floor below, or with wire loops threaded through the plaster and secured to the joists from above (Figs 32 and 33).

Where patches of external rendering must be removed, fill the horizontal surface of the remaining rendering below the gap and leave the edge weathered to throw the water off.

Bulges can be pinned back to the masonry by drilling through the bulge and putting plugs into the wall at 500–1000mm centres. Brass screws and brass gauze washers are then used to restrain the bulge and are set in lime putty and sand mixed 1:2 (Fig 34). In some circumstances large exposed washers of non-ferrous metal or exterior plywood would be adequate.

2.8.3 Wall and turret clocks

Clock mechanisms are invariably valuable, some very valuable. The

Fig 35 It was difficult to find a new user for the empty library in the centre of Bingley in 1982, but meanwhile it continued to contribute to the townscape; broken glass was always replaced and the clock told the right time

mechanism may be of any date between the fourteenth and mid twentieth century when turret clocks became electric and no more mechanical ones were made. The face is sometimes the least valuable part, being often a nineteenth- or twentieth-century repainting. The whole assembly is an important feature of the church, chapel, public building, stable block, market hall, clock tower, school, or station of which it forms a part.

The clock should be kept going if someone can be found to wind it. A clock telling the right time is a civic amenity and indicates that the building is being cared for (Fig 35). Local authorities pay for the upkeep of public clocks and they should be approached for help or for money, or possibly to see if they would wind the clock when they wind their own. The mechanism can be dangerous and the person winding the clock must have expert instruction; access can also be dangerous and repairing landings, ladders, and handrails is part of the necessary cost. The person who comes in weekly to wind the clock could be asked to report on other aspects of the building.

It may be worthwhile considering a permanent electric winding mechanism at the emergency repair stage. This involves specialist care and overhaul of the mechanism, and requires a 30 amp electricity supply to be maintained. The electric motor replaces the weights and the winding mechanism but nothing else. An electric clock to replace the old one deprives the building of an important historic feature, even if the previous face and hands remain.

Temporary measures to safeguard the clock mechanism pending full repair are as follows:

- A wooden case is needed to keep it clean. The old case could be repaired or a new one provided. Adequate space is needed inside for repair and maintenance.

- The weights should be let down and left down. If left in the up position they could fall and cause damage or injury.

- The mechanism must be oiled, but only with turret clock oil by someone who is reasonably expert. Over-oiling will not matter, but the oiling may have been neglected for some time already and a further period could cause irrevocable damage.

2.8.4 Organs

It is very easy to damage an organ and it may be the first target for vandals. The leather parts are a problem as they become brittle if the atmosphere is too dry and mouldy if it is too damp. The most valuable parts are the pipes.

Temporary protection is not easy and the best treatment is simply to maintain good ventilation and find someone to go in and play the organ as often as possible. This person will be a welcome user of the building and can be asked to keep an eye on other aspects of its condition.

Advice about the quality and value of an organ, or about the possibilities for selling it, can be obtained from the Redundancies Officer of the British Institute of Organ Studies.

See Appendix entry 24

If temporary repairs or protection are required the name of the most suitable local organ builder can be obtained from the Anglican Diocesan Organs Adviser.

2.9 External appearance

It has already been stressed that a well-tended appearance and an absence of rubbish are the best deterrents to vandals and fire raisers. A further reason for improving the appearance is to display the attractive qualities of the building to a potential purchaser or user.

If external painting is due, or overdue, it should be carried out both to preserve the stucco and the joinery and to present the building to its best advantage. Cleaning the masonry could even be considered after taking expert advice (see Case studies 7 and 12).

The same principle applies to surroundings and boundaries.

Physical boundaries in an urban situation are very important to a potential purchaser; they also play a vital part in the townscape. Nothing contributes more to an appearance of dereliction and neglect than broken fences and crumbling walls (Fig 36). These features are an invitation to intruders and those who dump rubbish. Front paths and gardens can be very inexpensively transformed and made to indicate that the building is cared for.

The local authority can be approached for a grant or other assistance towards permanent reinstatement of walls and railings abutting the highway or public footway. There may be an element of public safety involved, and they may have an interest in repairing their own adjoining surfaces. At the very least they may have a stock of matching railings, and they can be encouraged to support the repair of any historic features which are part of the townscape.

Fig 36 Unprotected houses and crumbling garden walls in listed Hanover Square, Bradford, downgraded the surrounding properties in 1982

3 Temporary uses for historic buildings

3.1 The need for temporary uses

An unused building is very likely to be at risk. There are dangers from intruders and vandals, damp and unnoticed leaks, sudden storm damage, birds in the roof space, lack of ventilation, and the cumulative effect of one item upon another. One way of guarding against these dangers is to find a suitable temporary user.

Temporary use is likely to cost less than maintaining the building empty; it will certainly cost less than a paid caretaker and it may even bring in a small income.

3.2 Obtaining vacant possession when required

The owner's main worry with short-term occupancy is the possible difficulty in obtaining possession when a permanent use is found. However, forms of agreement can be drawn up appropriate to all owners and types of property which ensure that a temporary occupier does not become a protected tenant. Such an agreement must be accompanied by a degree of trust and understanding between the owner and the occupier, because recourse to the courts runs counter to the whole idea of short-term use; the procedure itself takes too long and the costs are too high.

Expert advice is needed in the wording of the agreement but it need not be a lengthy document. As the purpose is to provide care for an historic building until certain circumstances arise, it is as well to say so in the agreement.

3.3 Payments and obligations for temporary use

A typical financial arrangement is that the user pays the rates but does not pay any rent. Even if the occupier pays a small rent, this is a less important consideration than his ability and willingness to care for the building.

The agreement can make it quite clear which repairs, if any, are to be carried out and by which party. The building must be kept or made weathertight and services must be provided. These items may be carried out by either party. Interior decorations and special fittings are almost always provided (with the owner's consent) by the user.

3.4 Care of valuable features

The valuable features of the building must be scheduled so that the user knows what he is supposed to be looking after and does not damage or alter them. Some historic buildings have a robust or much altered interior, which makes the schedule very short; in others many features may be listed, such as cornices, dado rails, door casings, doors and door furniture, window casings and shutters, panelling and cupboards, original floor boards, Victorian tilework, fire surrounds, and grates. It is important to mention everything because many people would not consider such things as, for example, plain panelled or boarded doors as being of special importance. It must be stipulated that previously unpainted items, such as hardwood, marble, or slate, may not be painted. The owner's access to check on specified items must be agreed, and the user's caretaking obligations must be specified.

3.5 Short-life housing

Housing is now a well-tried option for temporary use. An effective and reliable arrangement is to lease the property to a local housing association which has a proven record in managing short-term housing. The Empty Property Unit is a housing association which provides a comprehensive consultancy service to owners and users concerning the legal, financial, and managerial aspects of short-term use.

See Appendix entry 25

Another alternative is to negotiate directly with the local authority ensuring that they will undertake to rehouse their tenants at the end of the agreed term or period of notice.

An empty house in reasonably good condition can be leased for as little as six months, but when the users have to carry out works such as reroofing and providing services, they must have it for at least two or three years to make the repairs worthwhile. The occupants usually carry out the decorating if not the repairs. It is not unusual for occupants to take pride in the careful repair of an historic house; sometimes they take advantage of a local authority historic buildings grant to repair fully such items as railings and sash windows.

Short-life housing is usually shared accommodation, sometimes involving a small residents' cooperative. This is beneficial for an historic building as it avoids the necessity to divide a house into flats. The residents each have their own bedsitting room and share communal facilities. They pay enough to cover rates and running repairs and whatever rent has been agreed with the housing association or the owner. Low payments compensate for the lack of security of tenure and the unfinished condition of the accommodation.

3.6 Temporary shops

More and more charities are setting up shops to augment their funds.

Fig 37 Whilst this terrace in Calne waited for rehabilitation in 1987, the temporary use of one unit by a charity shop was of benefit to the building and the surroundings, in contrast to the boarded up unit next to it

If the historic building in question contains a frontage in a commercial location, there should be no difficulty in finding a charity who would like it. The owner would have to provide the basic services of water, tea-making facilities, a toilet, and a source of heat for winter complying with the Health and Safety at Work regulations. The charity would bring many benefits; they would probably be prepared to spend a reasonable sum on fitting out and painting the shop with the help of volunteers; they would also pay the rates, insure the shop window, and clean the glass. There is no reason why the agreement should not stipulate that the occupier makes a regular inspection of the whole building. The standard of shopfitting and display may not be very high, but the appearance will be much better than if the shop were boarded up (Fig 37). Sometimes the agreement includes a weekly fee, but more often the arrangement is no rent and no security of tenure. Charities will require an initial period long enough to give a possibility of recouping their outlay; after that the agreement could provide for as little as a week's notice to be given by either party.

To find a suitable charity, enquiries could be made at the local authority social services department or the Citizens' Advice Bureau; alternatively an advertisement could be placed in the local paper or the newsletter of the National Council for Voluntary Organisations. If the shop is in a good position, charities will compete for it.

See Appendix entry 26

3.7 Industrial and commercial uses

Owners of historic warehouses, factories, and agricultural and transport buildings often have particular difficulty in finding users. Years may elapse before a suitable use emerges and with it the finance for full repair. A free caretaking service could be of value during this period. If the 'caretaker' also used all or part of the building and paid the rates, the burden on the owner would be eased and the building would have a better chance of survival.

Temporary premises are suitable for new enterprises which will look for somewhere permanent as soon as their viability is established. They may be more willing to put in extra work (in caretaking and in making adaptations) than they would be to pay a normal rent. If a licence fee is agreed it should be suitably low to compensate for lack of security of tenure; it may involve no payment at all if the user were to carry out repairs. Alternatively, an agreement for a licence could be entered into whereby the licence did not come into effect until the repairs were done.

Temporary use of an historic building for light industry or craft workshops will very often involve a change of use. Planning authorities have now been directed to take a flexible attitude in the case of historic buildings, but if a permanent change is not considered desirable, consent could be given for a limited period. A primary need would be for the authority to avoid delay in giving their decision.

The two parties will have to apply jointly to the court to contract out of the protection which the law gives to business tenants. They will also have to contract out of the landlord's liability to pay compensation for improvements and disturbance. Obviously there are legal fees to be paid, but there is no need for long delays. In fact, if the matter is urgent, appointments for hearing these cases can be given at two or three days' notice.

To find a temporary user the local estate agents should obviously be contacted, but at the same time the county or district conservation officer or estates department may be able to help. Organisations such as the Rural Development Commission and Local Enterprise Agencies, where established, would be likely to be in touch with potential users.

See Appendix entry 27

3.8 Community uses

Any empty building which includes a room of reasonable size, or a hall, could be used for meetings, classes, discussion groups, or Women's Institute market societies. Accommodation is one of the main problems for local groups; schools have put up their charges for use of accommodation and church halls are often too big, too expensive to heat, or difficult to book for the required night.

For this kind of use the owner would have to provide minimum services, satisfy the local authority with regard to means of escape, and be responsible for essential repairs, but a voluntary organisation may be enthusiastic about caretaking for an historic building in return for its occasional use. Amongst a local group involved with the building there may be someone who passes it every day and would immediately report a broken window or a frozen hopper head.

The people to contact would be the same as those for temporary shops. In addition the Women's Institute may need accommodation for their monthly meetings or their market societies; the latter would need facilities to meet the statutory requirements for the selling of fresh food. They should be approached through the County Federation Office in the county or area in which the building is situated. Townswomen's Guilds have a wide variety of activities and regard themselves as a caring community of people, which is an attitude that certainly extends to the heritage. They should be contacted through the National Union of Townswomen's Guilds who will put the owner in touch with the most appropriate local people.

See Appendix entry 28

4 Examples of emergency repair

Listing status	Grade II
Local authority	South Oxfordshire District Council
Cost of emergency repair	1968, £200; 1974, £5000
Owner for full repair	Cabandale Ltd
Architect for full repair	Colin Bridger Dip Arch MSc RIBA MCIOB
Contractor for full repair	Boshers (Cholsey) Ltd
Cost of full repair	approx £200,000
Grants for full repair	DoE Section 10 £51,400; South Oxfordshire District Council and Wallingford Town Council £10,000
Awards	The RICS/The Times Conservation Award 1981; Civic Trust Commendation 1980

Case study 1: The Lamb Inn, Wallingford, Oxfordshire

Damage caused by ineffectual emergency repairs

Figs 38–43

This large inn had flourished on a prominent site at the heart of Wallingford since 1505. It stands at the central crossroads forming a familiar and distinguished feature which closes the view from the Market Place. The High Street side has a handsome early eighteenth-century facade of grey bricks, red dressings, and a generous segmental arch over the traditional entrance to the inn yard. The core of the building remains from the sixteenth century; along Castle Street is a later sixteenth-century timber-framed range with

Fig 38 The Lamb Inn, Wallingford: location plan

overhanging upper floors and twin gables. Beyond that is a Victorian addition with a bay window. In the centre the narrow coaching yard was flanked by stores and stables.

The inn has seen many distinguished visitors including William of Orange who stayed here in 1688 on his way from Abingdon to London to be crowned.

Fig 39 The Lamb Inn, Wallingford: ground floor plan, 1960

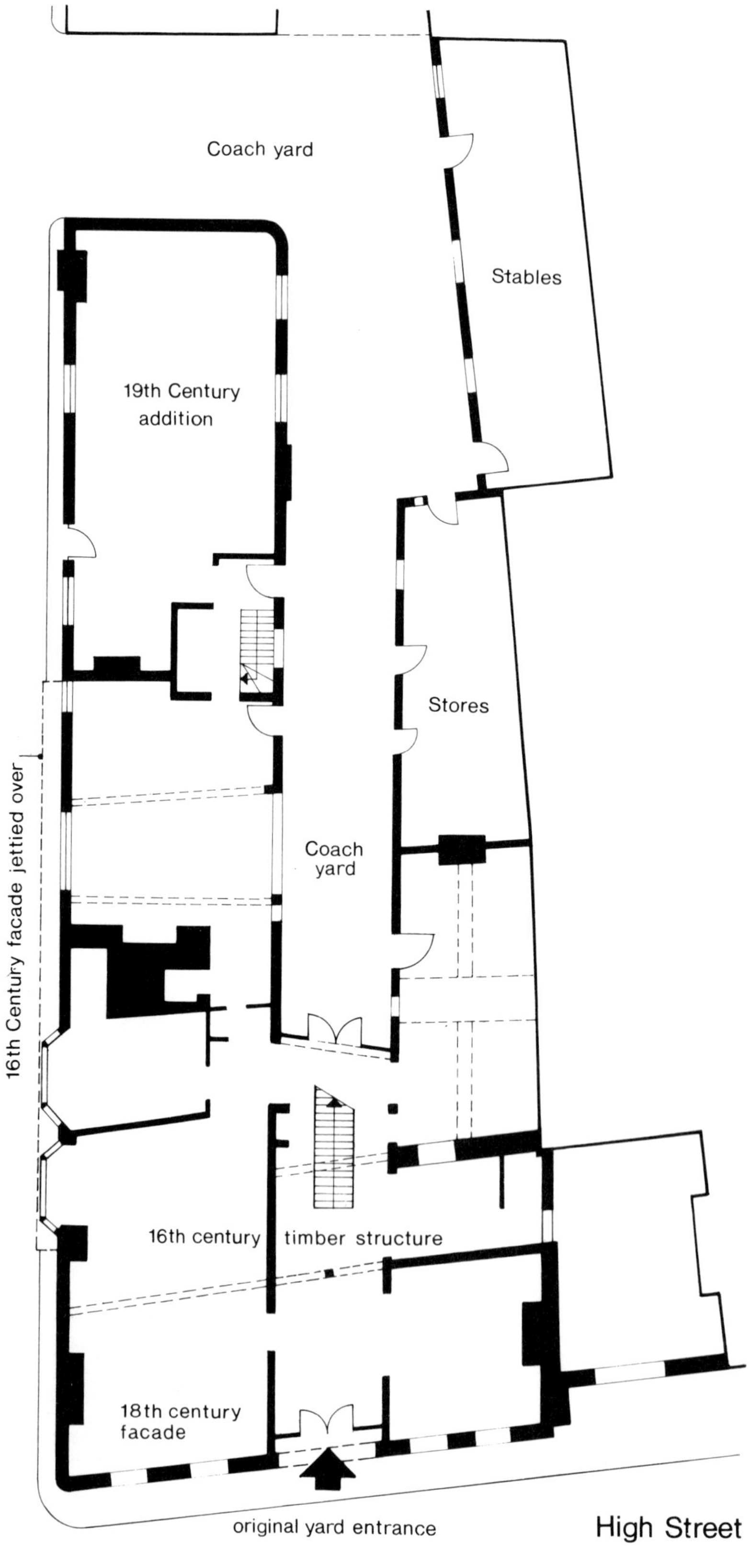

The causes of decay

From 1960 the building was no longer used as an hotel and its condition steadily deteriorated while a succession of owners sought for consent to use the site more profitably. Two applications for

Fig 40 The Lamb Inn, Wallingford: ground floor plan, 1981

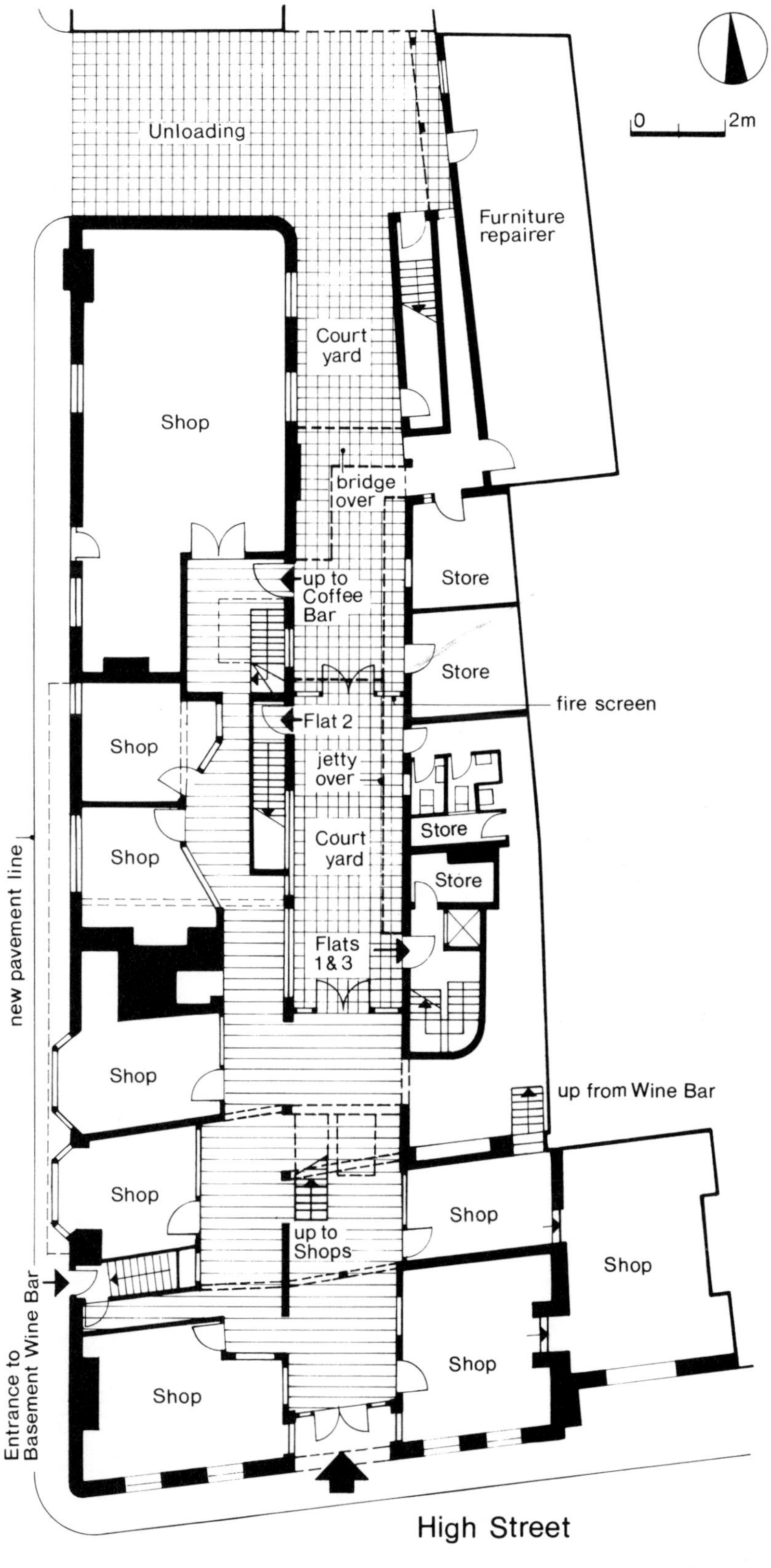

consent to demolish were refused. Five others for commercial schemes were approved but not implemented; this was due to the ever increasing requirements for repair and the pressure of traffic on the narrow streets, leading to access problems, lack of parking, and noise.

During this time it became what was described as 'a dangerous eyesore'. The slates on the High Street side began to slip and were a danger to passers-by. The jettied first floor of the Jacobean range was damaged by high-sided vehicles because of the very narrow footway below.

1968 and 1974: Emergency repairs

The first stage of emergency repair was carried out by the former Borough Council of Wallingford who stripped and felted the roof of the High Street range and recovered the cost from the owner. With hindsight it is clear that permanent reslating would have saved great sums of money in the future and preserved the historical integrity of the structure. In the event the felt was all the protection which the roof was to receive for the next ten years. It became torn and degraded and water poured in through the holes and at valleys and roof junctions.

Gradually the interior became unsafe and the front wall began to bow out due to rotting, and thus compression, of the horizontal

Fig 41 The Lamb Inn before repair in 1978, with support scaffold in position (photo: Colin Bridger)

Fig 42 The Lamb Inn, Wallingford: the sixteenth-century range in 1976 (photo: Colin Bridger)

timber binders which had originally been built into the inner face of the wall.

The second stage of emergency repairs in 1974 was an attempt, made at the instigation of the newly formed South Oxfordshire District Council, to stabilise the facade.

The pavement was much too narrow for raking shores and the wall was therefore propped internally with ties to an external scaffold. This treatment was ultimately ineffective and incidentally involved cutting through the main structural beams of the sixteenth-century frame.

1978–1980: Full repair

At last a company was formed locally on the initiative of Ann and Colin Bridger to repair the Lamb and to convert it to a two-level arcade for antique shops with a furniture repair workshop, a cafe, a basement wine bar, and flats on the upper floors. This scheme succeeded through the determination of local people to save a central symbol of their town and through their continuous detailed involvement in the process of conservation and conversion.

The architect made a coloured photographic survey of the front elevation and pasted the sections on hardboard to guide the bricklayer. The whole of the centre of the facade was then dismantled and rebuilt with the same bricks; only the segmental arch required

Fig 43 'The Lamb Arcade' in 1987

new bricks for reconstruction. The Jacobean range was repaired and its future integrity protected by the construction of a wide pavement with a higher kerb. The structural members which had been severed to make way for the internal shores were replaced by huge oak beams craned in through the roof, which then required complete reconstruction.

The whole building had become so decayed and ruinous that the rehabilitation was complicated and prolonged. A very high degree of detailed commitment and dedication was thus required and was provided by architect and builder alike.

Case study 2: 5–7 Elder Street, Spitalfields, London

Listing status	Grade II
Local authority	London Borough of Tower Hamlets
Owner at repair stages	The Spitalfields Historic Buildings Trust
Architect	Julian Harrap Dip Arch RIBA
Cost of emergency repair	£6500
Grant for emergency repair	DoE Section 10 £6500
Cost of full repair	£78,000
Grant for full repair	DoE Section 10 £44,200
Loan for full repair	Architectural Heritage Fund £30,000
Awards	The RICS/The Times Conservation Award 1981

Short-term emergency repair

Figs 44–53

Built about 1726, these houses were saved by the Spitalfields Historic Buildings Trust who were determined to halt the tide of demolitions and secure the future of the street in an historic housing area.

Although the external character is of the eighteenth century, this

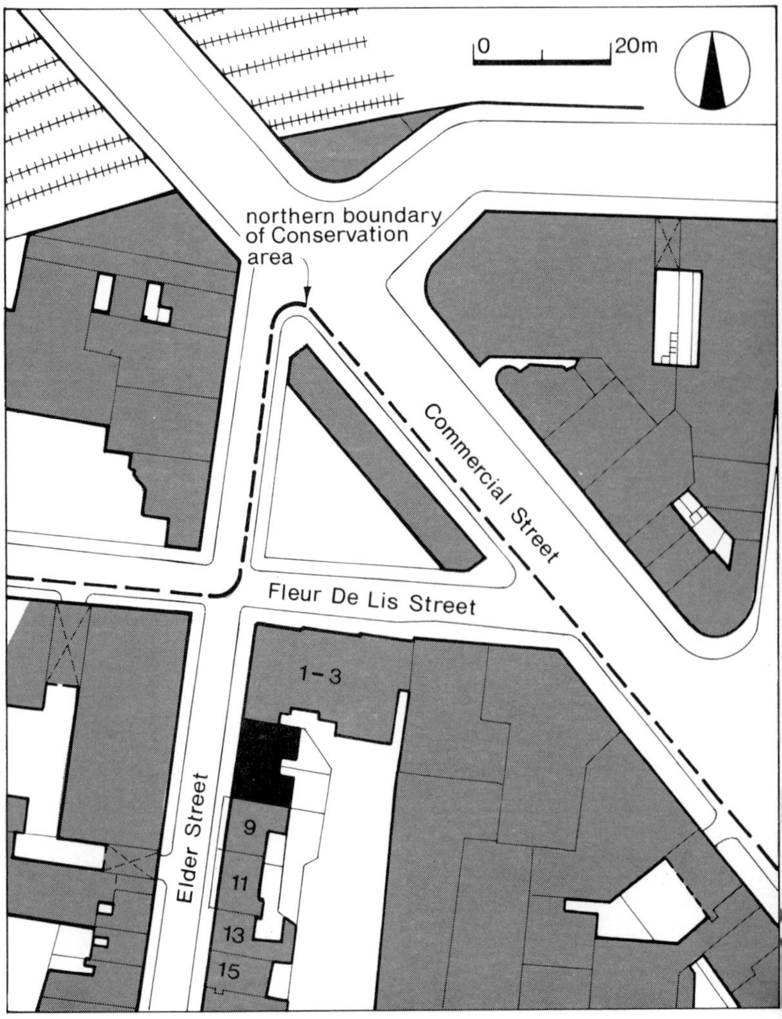

Fig 44 5–7 Elder Street, Spitalfields: location plan

Fig 45 5–7 Elder Street, Spitalfields: first floor plan

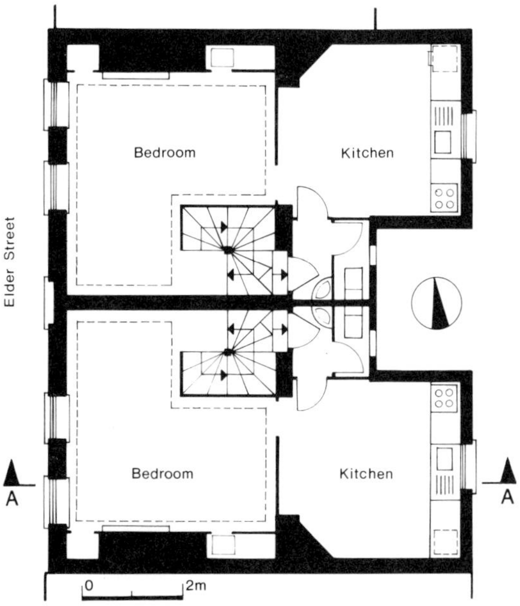

Fig 46 5–7 Elder Street, Spitalfields: Section AA

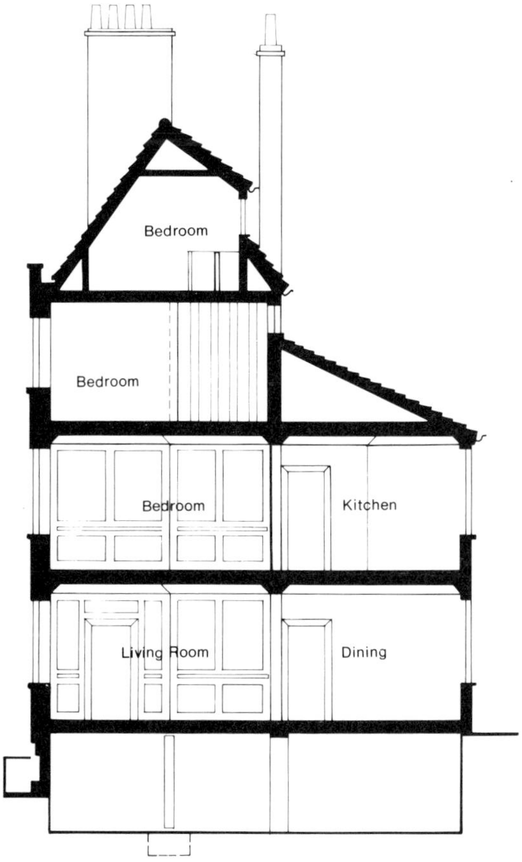

pair of houses has a plan type which is a rare medieval survival and was already archaic at the time of building. Each house is one room deep with a two-storey rear extension and a winding newel stair in the rear corner rising from basement to attic. At the back a cascade of roof slopes descends to small yards, and incorporates a leaded weaver's window and an original boarded attic wall.

The causes of decay

Because it was close to the City of London there was continuous pressure to redevelop the area. The houses had fallen into disrepair; they were the subject of three dangerous structure notices resulting in shoring by the previous owner, followed by removal of roofs and chimneys in preparation for demolition. Number 5 was roofless for six months and number 7 for two months. The historic panelling was very much at risk and the lime mortar in the walls was becoming saturated from the top leading to increased instability. The houses were stacked with decaying furniture, plaster, and rubbish. The basements were flooded as a result of severed water mains.

1978: Emergency repairs

First of all the buildings had to be saved from demolition and purchased. To this end individual members of the Trust occupied the derelict buildings, remaining in them by rota for 24 hours a day. Their determination brought success and the Trust then undertook emergency repairs while financial and contractural arrangements were made for complete repair.

Tarpaulins were immediately hired to cover the roof while preparations were made for scaffolding. The front elevation was leaning out by 123mm and settling at the sides; it was secured by a scaffold tied through the windows from front to back. The windows and shutters which had to be removed for this purpose were stored. The scaffold was extended to support a temporary corrugated iron

Fig 47 In 1978 an area of early eighteenth-century housing was threatened with demolition; numbers 5 and 7, seen here roofless, would have been the next to go in Elder Street (photo: Julian Harrap Architects)

Fig 48 5–7 Elder Street, Spitalfields: tarpaulins are being replaced by a protective scaffolding (photo: Julian Harrap Architects)

Fig 49 5–7 Elder Street, Spitalfields: an example of the condition of the original panelling which was saved as part of the emergency repairs (photo: Julian Harrap Architects)

Fig 50 5–7 Elder Street, Spitalfields: repaired panelling (photo: Julian Harrap Architects)

roof with a reinforced polythene skirt. The whole temporary structure was tied down with *in situ* concrete pads on the pavement and at the rear.

The scaffolding was hired for ten months. It allowed the structure to dry out during the pre-contract period and arrested the deterioration of the walls. It was known that the upper parts of the walls would have to be rebuilt, but it was argued that, if deterioration had been allowed to continue during the waiting period, lower levels of masonry would have become saturated and weakened and demolition would have become cumulative.

Permanent emergency repairs were needed to repair the cross wall and gable wall. These allowed the raking shores to be removed and the dangerous structure notice to be withdrawn.

After removing rubbish, disconnecting mains, securing the building, and pumping out the basements, a thorough conservation programme was undertaken. The panelling, shutters, and historic joinery were carefully removed and dried. A very detailed survey was made of the unstable and fractured brickwork of the facade; this made it possible to produce contour drawings revealing the pattern of movement. An eighteenth-century leaded light weaver's window was discovered, half complete under layers of hardboard and felt; this was removed for conservation.

1979: Full repair

Owing to the temporary restraint and the detailed surveying, only limited areas of the brick facades had to be rebuilt. All the conserved panelling and joinery were repaired and reinstated, a most painstaking process which was probably more expensive than making new work

Fig 53 The rehabilitation of numbers 5 and 7 has secured the end of the street (1987)

Fig 51 5–7 Elder Street, Spitalfields: the unusual roof formation giving rear light to the weaver's loft, rebuilt with original pantiles (photo: Julian Harrap Architects)

Fig 52 5–7 Elder Street, Spitalfields: original entrance doors in 1987

to match. However, the old work has the patina deriving from 250 years of continuous use and it gives the houses their historic domestic character. The weaver's window was reinstated. The part-framed floors were repaired rather than replaced.

Kitchens and bathrooms were located in rooms without wall panelling, but even here original fireplaces and panelled cupboards were retained. The attitude to repair was to remove cheap and makeshift additions but to repair late eighteenth- and early nineteenth-century modifications as well as the original features, and thus reveal the story of the houses.

Upon completion they were sold to private owners and became symbols of the much needed regeneration of the older parts of Spitalfields. The successful repair of two such badly decayed houses has encouraged owners to repair other neglected properties and no further demolition of listed buildings has taken place.

Listing status	Grade II
Local authority	Preston Borough Council
Owner at repair stages	Friends of Arkwright House
Architect	Niall Phillips BA Dip Arch (Bristol) RIBA, then of Form Structures Ltd, who undertook the work on a direct labour design and management contract
Cost of emergency repairs	Materials donated and labour voluntary; insurance premium £50
Cost of full repair	£252,750
Grants for full repair	DoE Section 10 £10,000; Preston Borough Council £10,000; Central Lancashire New Town Development Corporation £10,000; Charitable trusts and individuals approx £26,000; Manpower Services Commission schemes (including Skill Centre) £95,000 in labour costs
Loans for full repair	Architectural Heritage fund £35,000; Lloyds Bank loans and guarantees

Case study 3: Arkwright House, Preston, Lancashire

First aid repairs by volunteers

Figs 54–59

Arkwright House was built in 1728 as the residence for the headmaster of the nearby grammar school. In 1768 Richard Arkwright and his partner John Kay were renting a first floor room in the house. It was here, some time during that year, that they perfected the roller spinning device which came to be known as the spinning frame, and later as the water frame. This invention, which could be driven by water power, revolutionised cotton spinning and made possible the factory production methods which were at the heart of the industrial revolution.

The house is now the oldest in Preston. It is stuccoed on a stone base and contains two very fine panelled rooms and a staircase with dado panelling and pedimented arched openings. In the nineteenth century an extension containing shops was added on the east side. Further alterations took place in the twentieth century including removing the cross walls of the shops.

The position of the building near the Parish Church is environmentally important. It stands on the edge of an area which the local authority is now in the process of upgrading after a period of urban decline.

The causes of decay

In 1978 the building had been unused and deteriorating for about

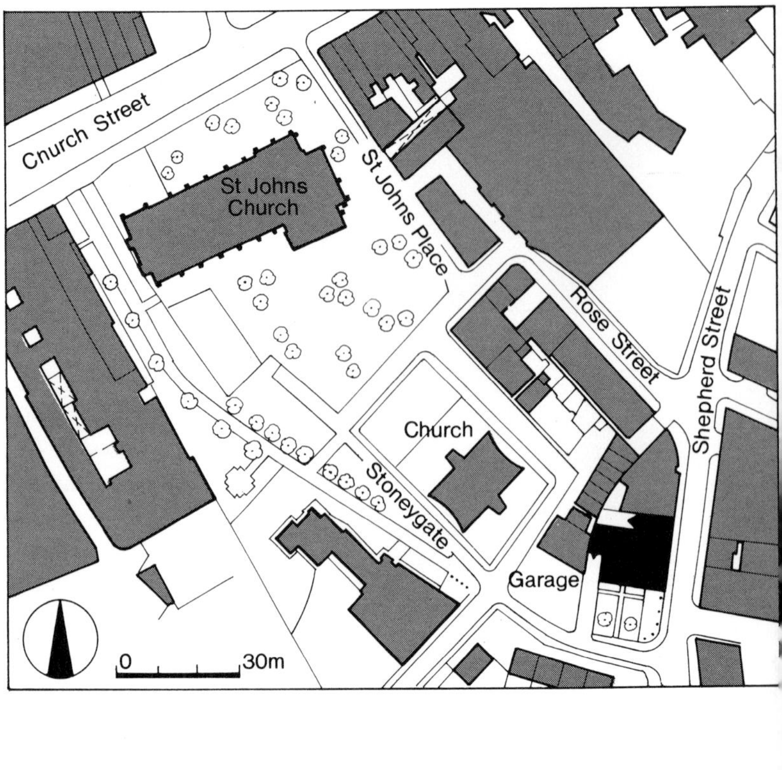

Fig 54 Arkwright House, Preston: location plan

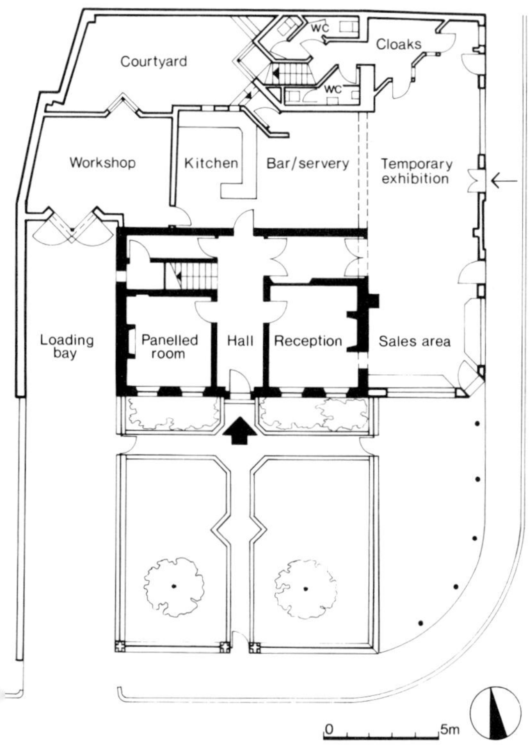

Fig 55 Arkwright House, Preston: ground floor plan

Fig 56 Arkwright House, Preston: first floor plan

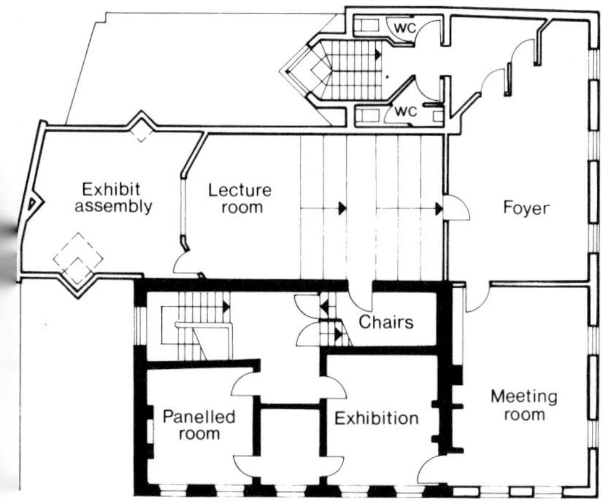

25 years; it had reached the state where much of the roof structure was collapsing and allowing severe water penetration. The twentieth-century timber beams replacing the cross walls had rotted through their bearing ends, leaving the east wall with no lateral support. In the original section of the building timber binders built into the walls had rotted, causing settlement.

The worst problem was the lack of doors and windows, which enabled vandals to get in. They were stripping out panelling and other valuable items and constituting a serious fire risk.

The owner of the building was an elderly, infirm lady who had no interest in its maintenance or repair. Dealings with her had to be through her solicitor.

1978: Emergency repairs

In spite of an application for listed building consent to demolish the building, the local planning officers encouraged the Friends of Arkwright House to attempt a rescue operation.

A group of volunteers from the Friends carried out the following works themselves:

- Sealing the rooflights with polythene sheets.
- Covering the damaged areas of roof with tarpaulins, which was done by pushing them through the roof lights and over the ridge and tying them down at the eaves on the opposite side.
- Removing to a secure place valuable items such as stair balusters, damaged panelling, and joinery sections.
- Clearing out rubbish and debris to allow the fabric to dry and to improve its appearance.
- Sealing upper floor windows with polythene fixed with battens to frames.
- Sealing ground floor windows with plywood and corrugated iron.
- Propping two beams in the nineteenth-century part using baulks of timber already on site.

The work was undertaken by voluntary labour organised by the Friends of Arkwright House with the agreement of the owner. It attracted much attention in the local press and most materials were donated. Ladders and tarpaulins were loaned by Form Structures Ltd who supervised the work. Skilled work was not required and the volunteer labour was thus quite adequate. The only significant cost was the heavy insurance premium for the volunteers.

These repairs had to remain effective for about 12 weeks. The building was thus protected from vandals, made largely waterproof, and allowed to dry out until the next stage of work became possible. Having demonstrated their determination in a practical way the Friends were able to obtain financial help for full repair.

Fig 57 Arkwright House open to vandals in 1978 (photo: Architectural Heritage Fund)

1978–1980: Full repair

Fig 58 Arkwright House, Preston: meticulously repaired panelling and a newly designed fire surround (photo: Architectural Heritage Fund)

The Friends of Arkwright House commissioned an ambitious scheme for the complete repair and conservation of the building for museum and educational uses. A new extension was built for workshops and storage; facilities were provided for adult education conferences and lectures. Panelling and staircase details were meticulously repaired; new work was designed to be identified both in planning and detailing by a diamond theme. Tie rods, with commemorative tie plates, were installed to stabilise the east elevation. The forecourt garden and railings were recreated.

Eight years later

When the building work was complete the Lancashire County Council used the house rent-free as an adult education centre, covering all the running costs. The Friends of Arkwright House coordinated an appeal to clear the outstanding loans. They hoped

Fig 59 Arkwright House, Preston: rehabilitation completed in 1981; by 1987 the local authority had begun to upgrade the area between the house and the church (photo: Architectural Heritage Fund)

that the county council would eventually lease the building and use it for the educational and museum purposes for which it was converted.

By 1986 the Friends had not been able to repay their loans and the county withdrew from its use of the building. The mortgage receivers put the building on the market and it once again faced an uncertain future until in 1988 it was bought by a charitable organisation.

Case study 4: Houses in Gillygate, York

Saving an historic street

Figs 60–76

Gillygate is a narrow street immediately outside the city wall of York. It follows the line of the wall and is close to the bottom of the steep slope which climbs to the base of the ramparts. The street has been lined with housing since the fifteenth century but what can now be

Listing status	6 houses Grade II; 20 houses unlisted
Local Authority	City of York
Architects for emergency repair	City of York Architects Department
Cost of emergency repair	Approx £15,500 for 12 properties
Grants for emergency repair	DoE Section 10 £11,700 for 10 properties
Architects for full repair	Various firms working for prospective buyers in association with the conservation team of the City of York Planning and Estates Department, led by June Hargreaves MBE MUniv (York) DipTP MRTPI, Assistant City Planning Officer (Development Control and Conservation)
Cost of full repair	Mainly borne by prospective purchasers. Public funding may be found to be less than the £500,000 transferred to Gillygate capital reserve account in 1977. Town Scheme for 67 houses operated for ten years and paid a total of £190,192 matched by central government. County council contribution was in the form of the houses they owned. Improvement grants and Section 10 grants were paid for some houses but the city council received the proceeds from the sale of properties upon completion of work.

seen is eighteenth-, nineteenth-, and early twentieth-century buildings. The result is a remarkably homogeneous brick-built street full of interesting variations. Its character, and its fluctuating fortunes, have derived from its special position as an historic thoroughfare leading to Bootham Bar and thence directly into the city and to the Minster.

There are 72 properties in Gillygate, out of which this study covers numbers 1–26 at the south end. Six of these are listed Grade II.

The causes of decay

Professor Adshead's 1948 plan for York proposed removing the properties from the moats outside the city walls (including the east side of Gillygate) and forming a green swathe encircling the walled city. Traffic considerations were secondary to the appealing idea of opening up fine views of the walls, with the Minster above them.

However traffic was, and is, a major problem and the proposed removal of the houses on the east side of Gillygate provided an opportunity for successive traffic schemes to be considered; these included the widening of the street and the demolition of more houses on the west side to provide access to a multi-storey car park. Meanwhile the city and the county were buying the houses in order to facilitate the implementation of whichever plan was finally adopted. A period of uncertainty extended over 25 years but, even so, a brief survey in 1970 designated only numbers 23 and 25 out of the 26 buildings as being derelict and only five houses as needing attention.

In 1973 Eric Pearson, the city planning officer, produced a

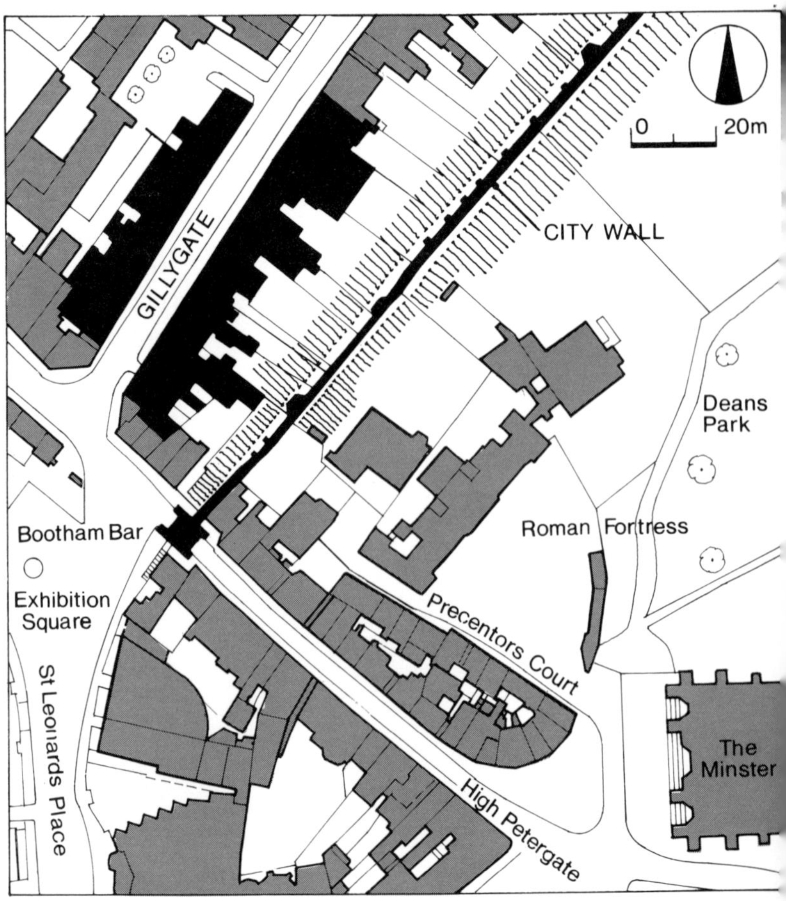

Fig 60 Gillygate, York: location plan

reappraisal of the area including a townscape study of the now rapidly decaying street; he questioned whether it was aesthetically desirable to open up the one remaining unexposed length of city wall, and whether this particular part of the current traffic scheme was necessary or cost-effective.

Public opinion was veering more and more strongly towards conservation, and in 1977 the city council decided to restore Gillygate by means of a Town Scheme. By this time 24 out of 26 houses were in various critical stages of disrepair and the street had reached its lowest ebb. £500,000 was set aside by the council for the rehabilitation of the street, the county council donated the properties it had bought in lieu of financial contribution, and the slow climb back to a viable and living street began.

1976–1978: Emergency repairs

A job creation scheme was used to clear the rubbish between the backs of the houses and the city wall; this was important to improve the view from the popular walk around the walls.

Time was bought and decay arrested in the years 1977 to 1978. The City began to protect those buildings which it owned by treating the dry rot, boarding up windows, reroofing, attending to rainwater goods, and making the buildings safe. Unfortunately the conservation team had very little control over the extent of these works and none over work to unlisted buildings. Greater protection might have been given at this stage and more historic features could possibly have been saved.

Of the 26 houses covered by this study, 17 had been bought for clearance by the city or county councils; 13 of these and one privately-owned house were given emergency repairs. These measures preserved the street intact so that no new infill would become necessary.

1978–1987: Full repair

The city council was now determined to have the houses well repaired. There was to be no question of rebuilding behind repaired facades as this was to remain a genuine historic street. Tenders were invited for the eventual purchase of city-owned houses. Town Scheme and housing improvement grants were offered for all houses and Section 10 grant was available for some. The city-owned houses were temporarily leased upon approval of the schemes submitted and no sale was allowed until the work on the property was finished. A time limit was negotiated for completion of repairs and a penalty imposed for overrunning the time.

The Town Scheme was in operation from 1978 to March 1987. When it came to an end all the houses in this study were repaired. All the ground floors were shops or restaurants and only two were temporarily empty. Even the upper floors, which are frequently a problem, were nearly 90% occupied. The street did not have the appearance of a tourist show piece; it looked, and was, part of the living fabric of the city.

This achievement represents 11 years of continuous work. Some of the factors which contributed to its success were as follows:

Fig 63 Gillygate, York: numbers 3 and 5 before repair (photo: York City Council)

Fig 64 Gillygate, York: numbers 3 and 5 in 1987

- The emergency repairs ensured that the objective of retaining a continuous, genuinely historic street could be achieved.

- The unique leasing system ensured that the conservation team could control the quality of historic rehabilitation.

- Unlike in the centre of York, rents are within the means of small businesses.

- The route, as always in the past, attracts pedestrians who now walk along it from car parks to the city centre and thus ensure the viability of the shops.

- The conservation team had the same skilled and dedicated leader for the whole period of rehabilitation.

Numbers 3 and 5

These comprise the first pair on the west side. They have a very interesting upper elevation, now painstakingly restored to an original design of 1797. They were built by Thomas Wolstenholme, a prolific maker of composition ornaments with which he lavishly decorated the interiors. The emergency repairs were just in time to ensure their survival and to check destruction by squatters who were burning stair balusters for firewood. The pair of houses has been converted horizontally into three flats with two shops below. The second staircase has been retained as a required alternative means of escape from the upper floors. Nothing survived of the original ground floor facade and this is now a new design.

Numbers 23 and 25

The last of the group on the west side was an eighteenth-century house remodelled around 1800 as two dwellings with double height bay windows and timber door cases with reeded columns and open pediments. These were among the earliest to be bought by the city council for clearance and they were designated derelict in 1970. They were made watertight by emergency repairs in 1976 and the windows were boarded up.

However, a repair scheme was not approved until 1982 and six years of waiting proved to be too long; one of the door cases disappeared and the boarding was not fully effective in keeping out intruders. The emergency repairs prevented total loss but they did not enable the architecture to play its part in upgrading the street during the waiting period.

The houses now stand at the entrance to a thriving subsidiary rehabilitation behind numbers 3–25. Cafe, restaurant, shops, and workshops have a view of the repaired backs which have received no less care than the street elevation and present a typical historical amalgam of gables and additions.

Fig 65 Gillygate, York: numbers 23 and 25; work beginning in 1982 after six years of temporary repair (photo: York City Council)

Fig 66 Gillygate, York: numbers 23 and 25 in 1983, also showing the entrance to a lively rehabilitation behind (photo: York City Council)

Fig 67 Gillygate, York: number 26 in 1980 (photo: York City Council)

Fig 68 Gillygate, York: the back of number 26 as seen from the city wall in 1980 (photo: York City Council)

Fig 69 Gillygate, York: the back of number 26 in 1981 (photo: York City Council)

Number 26

Built in 1769 by Robert Clough, bricklayer and master mason, this is one of a pair of large listed houses on the east side of the street. The back elevation, together with that of number 28, is prominently visible from the city wall. Large round-headed windows light the staircases and both houses have a small projecting closet wing, three storeys high. Number 26 was bought for demolition by the county council but received grant aid and emergency repairs in 1977. The house was then made secure, dry rot was dealt with and prevented from spreading to the adjoining house, roof trusses were plated and strutted, and the house made watertight. The rot made it necessary to remove some of the panelling and door cases but they were first photographed, thus providing evidence which was essential at the repair stage.

A buyer came forward for this house and shop and it was repaired and sold in 1981. The original window designs have been reinstated on both sides and the removal of twentieth-century additions has enhanced the rear view from the city wall.

Fig 70 Gillygate, York: number 26 in 1987

Fig 71 Gillygate, York: numbers 16–20 in 1979; they remained the worst problem of the street until the shell was repaired by the City Council (photo: York City Council)

Numbers 16, 18, and 20

This was an early eighteenth-century, two-storey house, built on an L-shaped plan with a width of seven windows facing the street. In the early nineteenth century a third storey was added and the house divided into two. In more recent times the ground floor became three shops.

This block was the main problem of the street; the houses were owned by the city council and became so poor in condition that only the existence of the Town Scheme tipped the balance against demolition. Initially emergency repairs were mainly dry rot treatment by a specialist firm. A great deal of timber was removed and the houses became virtually gutted and roofless with floors and staircases removed and outer walls deprived of restraint. A second stage of emergency repairs was needed in 1982 due to the threatened collapse of half the front elevation. An inner structure was then built to which the elevation was tied.

The conservation officer would have preferred a much less drastic approach in which dry rot would have been checked but the historic features left ready for repair. In this way the houses would have been more viable and attractive to prospective purchasers.

In their gutted condition no one would buy the houses except for demolition and rebuilding, but the council was still determined that the original fabric should remain, equal importance being attached both to the back and to the front. Therefore they carried out permanent emergency repairs to roof and external walls and the group was bought by a builder who converted it into shops and flats.

Fig 72 Gillygate, York: the backs of numbers 16–20 seen from the city wall in 1977 (photo: York City Council)

Fig 73 Gillygate, York: numbers 16–20 in 1987, with the seven first floor windows showing the extent of the original early eighteenth-century house

Fig 74 Gillygate, York: a view from the city wall in 1984 after repairs (photo: York City Council)

Fig 75 The east side of Gillygate in 1987, looking towards Queen Margaret's Arch

Fig 76 The west side of Gillygate in 1987

Numbers 4 and 6

This pair of houses is a splendid example of late Victorian architecture by W Penty. Owned by the city council, they received grant aid for emergency repairs in 1977. The new owner carried out the full repairs himself in close cooperation with the city's conservation team. He had a turnery and pottery at the back of the house and used his own skills to make matching turned balusters and moulded bricks for the damaged and idiosyncratic elevation. The work was finished in 1982.

The new use is two shops with a guest house above, and guests will find all the late nineteenth-century details repaired and cleaned, including cast iron fireplaces with inset tiles, stained glass, cornices, joinery, and a fine staircase with a minstrels' gallery.

Listing status	Unlisted
Local authority and owner	Bolton Metropolitan Borough Council
Architect	Anthony Pass BA BArch (Manchester) RIBA, of Greater Manchester Council Architectural Services Unit
Cost of emergency repair	Approx £2500
Cost of full repair	£132,400
Grant for full repair	Countryside Commission £37,150

Case study 5: Rock Hall, Farnworth, Bolton, Lancashire

The problems of an isolated historic building

Figs 77–81

This is a small manor house built around 1820–1840 for John Crompton who was a local papermill owner. The Crompton family built the first papermills in Lancashire and their name was given to the adjoining lodges (manmade lakes). Rock Hall stands above the lodges in a prominent elevated position overlooking the river Croal. It has seen the evolution of the land from countryside to industry, later to dereliction, and in the 1970s to reclamation. This was implemented by the Joint Reclamation Team of the Greater Manchester Council and has created the linear parkland of the Croal Irwell Valley, with the Moses Gate Country Park at its centre.

The brown brick house has a comfortable expansive appearance with a wide pediment, a broad, round-headed doorway, and nine large windows. Its former grade III listing was deleted from the updated schedules because of the damage and deterioration it had suffered.

Fig 77 Rock Hall, Farnworth: location plan

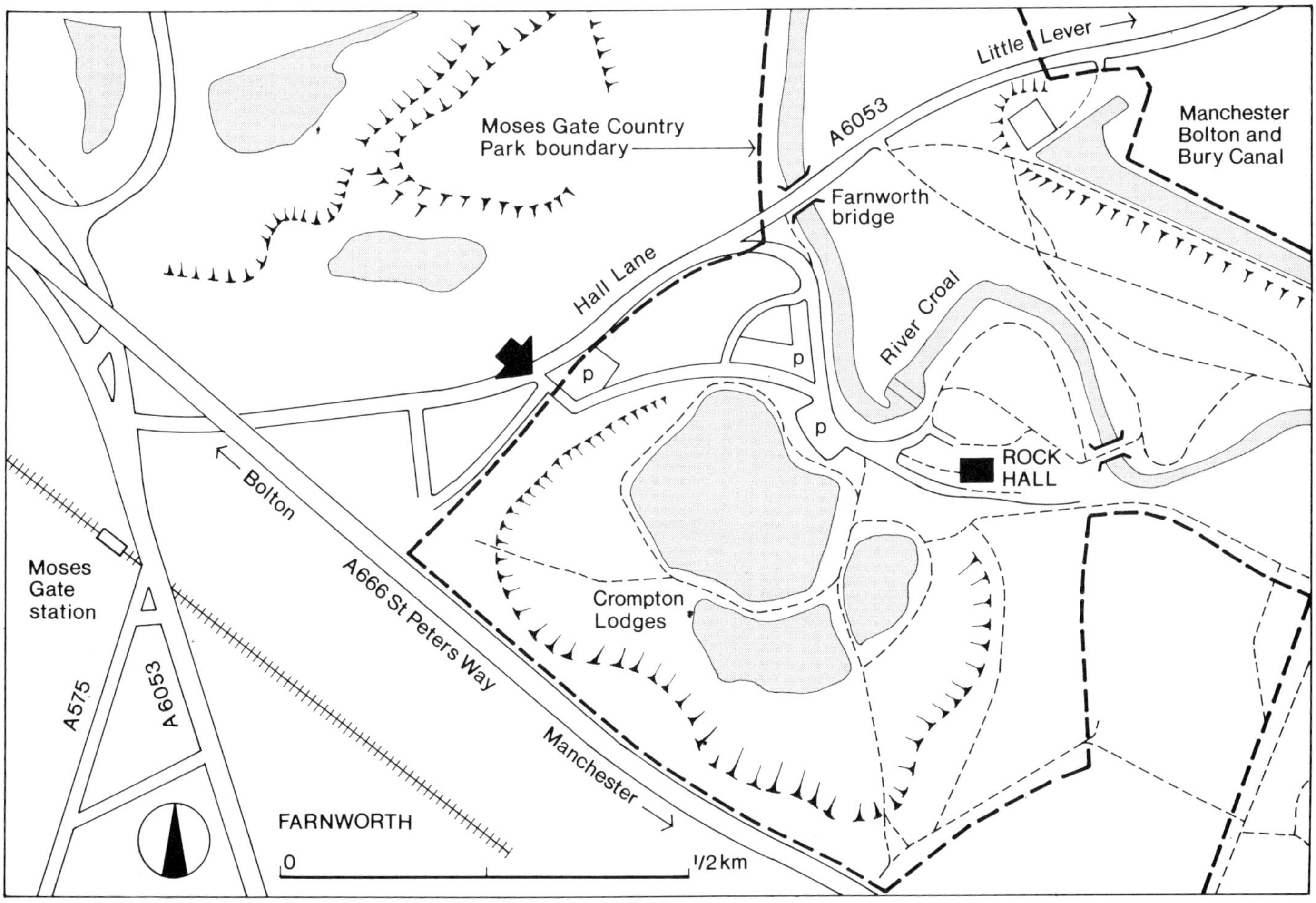

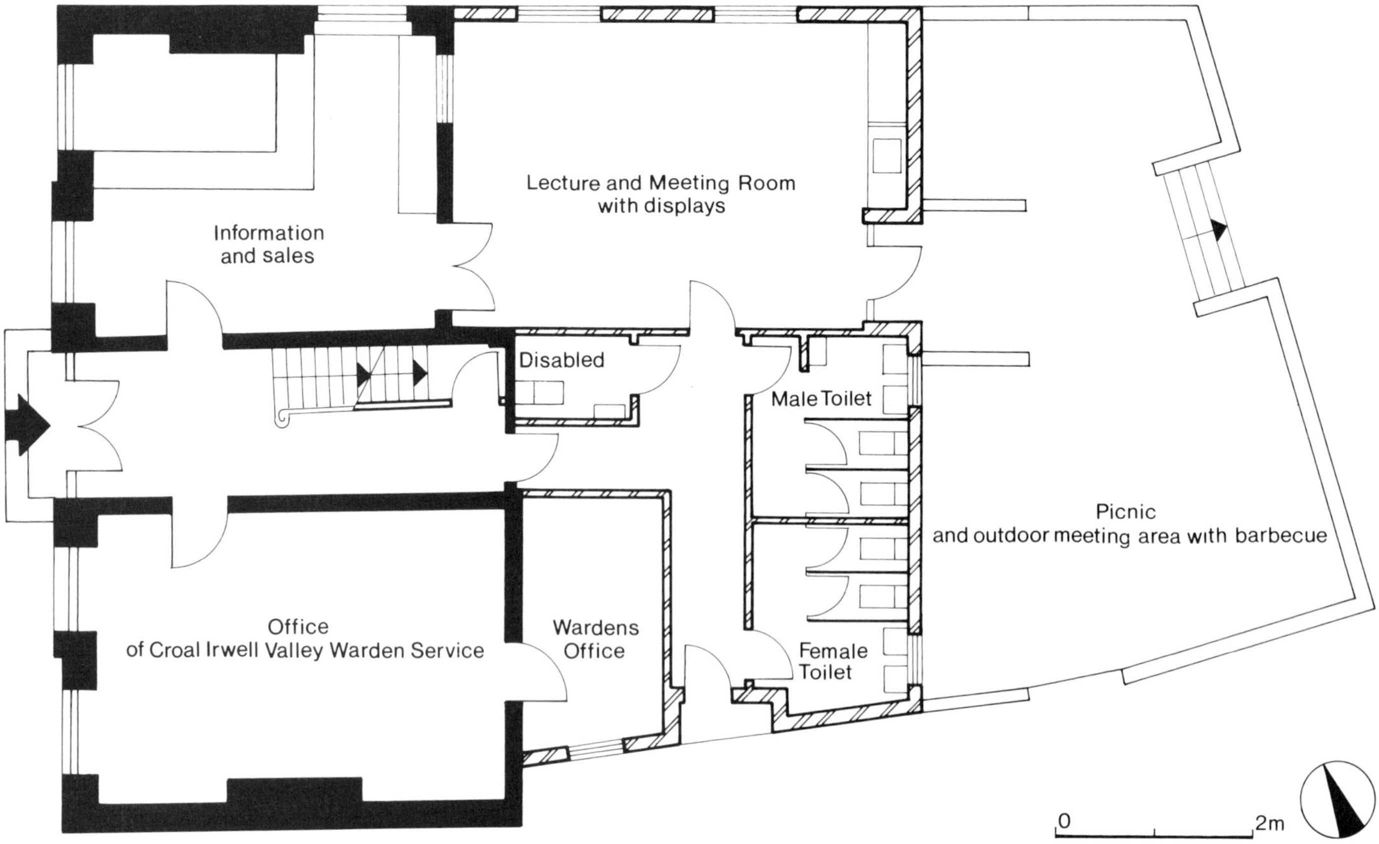

Fig 78 Rock Hall, Farnworth: ground floor plan

Fig 79 Rock Hall, Farnworth: basement and first floor plan

The causes of decay

The building had been acquired by the Bolton housing department who divided it into two flats. Its condition continued to deteriorate and when the tenants moved out it remained vacant from 1976 to 1980. Vandalism and water penetration intensified the problems of general neglect and the building's future was very uncertain.

1976–1980: Emergency repairs

Several repair operations took place during this time, including patching the roof and mending the gutters. The windows and doors were infilled with brickwork which was not entirely successful; it was penetrated at least once by vandals in spite of the use of a strong mortar, which damaged the arrises of the reveals when it was removed. A structural survey revealed an urgent need to take down a dangerous chimney stack.

1980–1981: Full repair and conversion

Plans for the Croal Irwell Valley and the Moses Gate Country Park included a requirement for a warden base and visitor centre with a warden's flat. Not everyone concerned thought that Rock Hall would provide the ideal building, but the fact that it had been saved won

Fig 80 Rock Hall under emergency repair (photo: A J Pass)

support for it and the conversion took place. Only the front section survives, including the cellars which provide essential tool storage and a warden's workshop. The back was rebuilt and a single storey extension added.

Six years later

The house is now a thriving centre of innumerable countryside activities from the study of rural history and archaeology to guided walks, bird watching, kite flying, and the children's 'Watch club'. The three lodges are separately used for boating, wild life, and fishing. The meadow between the house and the river is being made into a wild flower reserve. The information room provides such things as country park newsletters, wildlife fact sheets, and walkers' maps. The meeting room contains displays and is used by school children on weekdays, for lectures in the evenings, and by the public at weekends. Rock Hall, once isolated in a wasteland of industrial dereliction, now serves a useful purpose and provides the new park with an historic feature.

Fig 81 Rock Hall, Farnworth, in 1988 (photo: English Heritage)

Listing status	Grade II
Local authority	Cheltenham Borough Council
Cost of emergency repair	£1580
Grant for permanent emergency repair	£213 from the borough council
Owner for full repair	Pillar Aluminium Ltd
Architects for full repair	Stanley Partnership Cheltenham
Cost of full repair	£96,000
Grant for full repair	DoE Section 10 £41,600
Cost with new extension	£727,000

Case study 6: 113–115 Bath Road, Cheltenham, Gloucestershire

The determination of the planning authority saves a Regency elevation

Figs 82–87
Amongst a wealth of Regency architecture in Cheltenham, this pair of villas is unique. They were built around 1825 following the extension of the Bath Road southwards. At various periods they have been the homes of a series of clergymen and have also been leased by Cheltenham College.

The corner porches are projected forward and linked by a continuous balcony supported on four Ionic columns. The principal upper windows are three light sashes with cornices and long console brackets. The pair is united by a hipped slate roof and central chimney. The front elevation is faced with very finely detailed stonework.

The causes of decay

The site on the Bath Road gradually became less desirable for

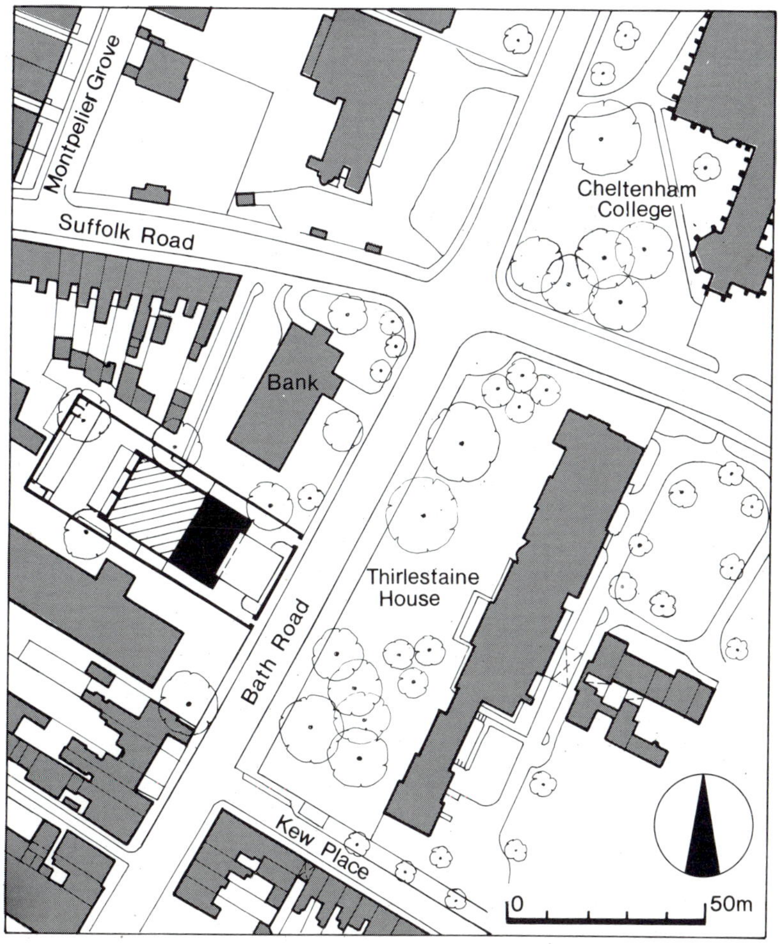

Fig 82 113–115 Bath Road, Cheltenham: location plan

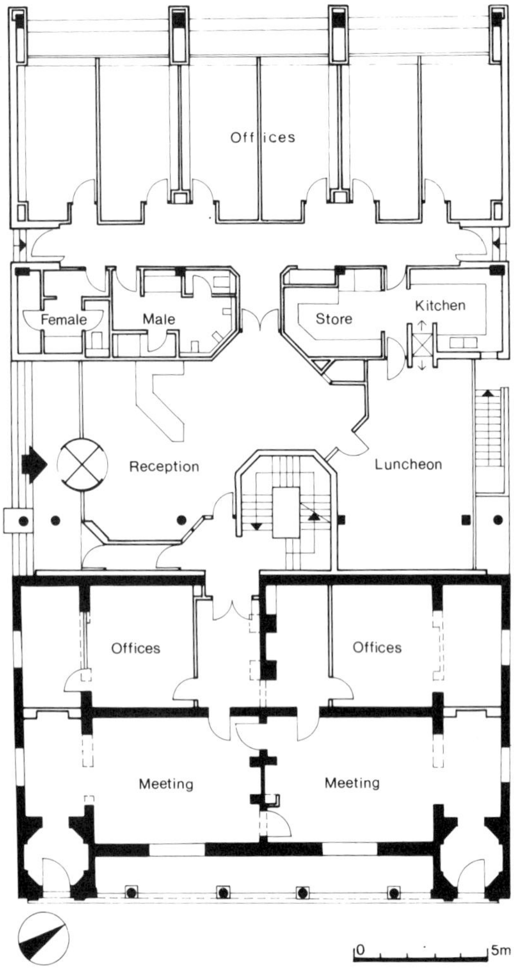

Fig 83 113–115 Bath Road, Cheltenham: above, ground floor plan; below, first floor plan

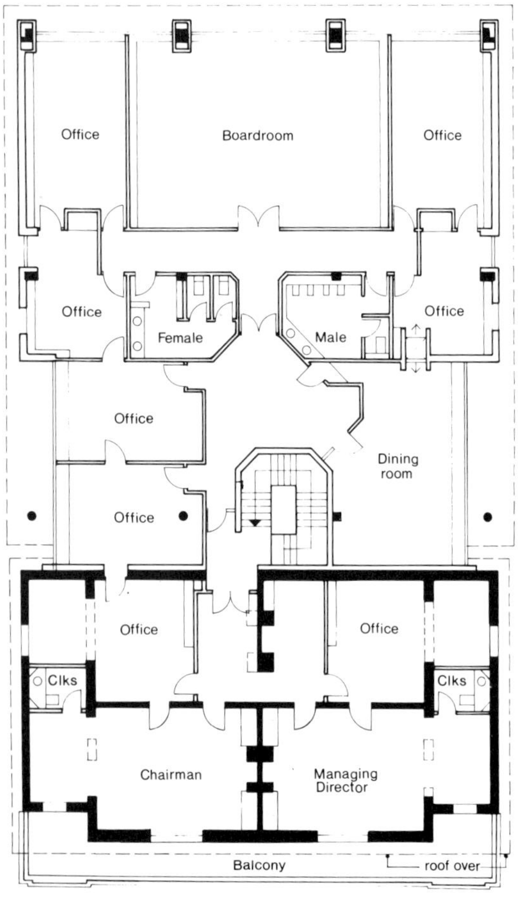

Fig 84 113–115 Bath Road, Cheltenham in 1975 (photo: Cheltenham Borough Council)

residential purposes, and at the same time potentially profitable for office or commercial use. The pair of houses was therefore the subject of a 13-year dispute between the owner and Cheltenham Borough Council. From 1966 to 1978 the planning history is of four applications to demolish and one appeal, all refused; one application for office use of the existing building was approved but not implemented. In 1972 the houses became vacant and remained so, being intermittently vandalised and used by vagrants, until 1979 when the contractors moved in. In 1978 number 113 was partly gutted by fire.

An architect's survey in 1975 recorded a long catalogue of defects including numerous attacks of dry rot, theft of lead ridges and hips, missing rainwater goods, structural cracks, leaning chimneys, settlement, rotted windows, smashed glass, missing rendering and copings, collapsed timber lintels and ceilings, saturation of walls, vandalised joinery details, and, worst of all, damage to the Ionic columns and the front door stonework of number 113 whose stone balustrade was completely missing. The stonework of number 115 had not fared much better as it had been treated with a cement paint and the leadwork of the balcony above had been removed.

1975: Emergency repairs

These were carried out by the owner as the result of a Section 101 notice. Temporary repairs included felt covering to gutters and balcony, boarding up of windows, clearing of debris and vegetation, spraying of dry rot with fungicide, and patch repair of some of the subsidiary roofs. Permanent emergency work comprised reslating the main roof.

The work arrested decay for only about one year. The boarding up was doubly unsatisfactory in that it was not only ineffective but also made use of the internal doors which were thus destroyed.

1979: Full repair

Consent was given in 1978 for office use, which involved more than doubling the area by building a rear extension, but retained the front section of the original building. The first contract included a completely new roof, underpinning, filling the basement, rebuilding the balcony, restoring the stonework, and providing new windows and external doors. Towards the end of the year the new leaseholders were able to buy the freehold and began work on a new design for the interior and the extension, which provided 13,000 square feet of office space.

Fig 85 Bath Road, Cheltenham: the stonework of number 115 had been covered with cement paint (photo: Cheltenham Borough Council)

Fig 86 Bath Road, Cheltenham: number 113, overwhelmed with vegetation, and progressively losing the finely detailed stonework (photo: Cheltenham Borough Council)

Seven years later

The new freeholders are very pleased with their Regency facade, which is all that can be seen from the road of their prestigious company headquarters. They admit that they were not looking for an historic building but they wished to be in Cheltenham and could not find a suitable vacant site. Now they have adopted the elegant elevation as a very up-market symbol on the brochure of their 20 companies.

Nothing actually remains of the original pair of villas except the main structural brick walls and the facade which is largely recreated. The emergency repairs were too late and too ineffectual; nevertheless, without them the building might well have been demolished and commercial buildings would have pressed further into Regency Cheltenham.

Fig 87 113–115 Bath Road, Cheltenham: the restored elevation in 1988 concealing the large office extension behind it (photo: English Heritage)

Case study 7: Warehouse, Liverpool Road Station, Manchester

The problems of a very large historic structure

Figs 88–97

The definitive assessment of this warehouse has been made by R S Fitzgerald in his historical and architectural survey of Liverpool Road Station.* The book was published in 1980 during the 150th anniversary of this, the oldest surviving purpose-built railway station in the country, and possibly in the world. A fascinating story is told of how this prototype passenger and goods station came into being as a terminus of the first mainline railway.

*Published by Manchester University Press in association with the Royal Commission on Historical Monuments and the Greater Manchester Council.

The warehouse has brick walls and a massive internal timber frame. Amazingly, it survived in use until 1976 and Fitzgerald concludes that, as far as is known, nothing comparable to it still stands. Four bays of the structure are virtually unaltered since initial changes in 1831. Two-inch floor boards, bridging joists, 13-inch square main beams, timber storey posts, cast iron columns in the cellar, stair towers, roof trusses, and lifting gear all remain. The only significant change took place in 1860 when the internal rails were removed and the floor levelled off at platform height.

The plan is divided into five major compartments indicated on the elevations by ten gables. Four compartments are paired and handed and the eastern one is divided. The symmetrical arrangement of rail entries and stairs for each pair produces perfectly logical elevations of great subtlety.

The storey height drop between rail level and carting level facilitated the transfer of goods. In the centre bay the trains could originally pass right through the building and over a bridge to two more warehouses beyond.

Listing status	Grade II*
Local authority	Manchester City Council
Owners for 1980 emergency repair	British Rail followed by Greater Manchester Metropolitan County Council
Architect for 1980 emergency repair	Anthony Pass BA BArch RIBA, Conservation Officer, Greater Manchester Council
Cost of 1980 emergency repair	£60,000 provided by the Greater Manchester Council and the Inner Cities Fund
Present owner	Greater Manchester Museum of Science and Industry Trust
Architect for the National Electricity Gallery	Thomas Worthington & Sons
Architect for 1988 emergency repair	Ken Moth of Building Design Partnership
Cost of 1988 emergency repair	£35,000 from Museum funds

The causes of decay

British Rail stopped using the warehouse in 1976 but two years passed before it was actually bought by the Greater Manchester Council. It was in a deplorable condition with a very poor appearance; the condition of the slates was too bad for eventual reuse, the valley gutters leaked, the stone gable copings were seriously damaged, and the brickwork was disfigured with deteriorating paint. The worst result of these external defects was deterioration of the timber structure due to water penetration.

1977–1980: Emergency repairs

The Greater Manchester Council was considering the future of the building as part of a long-term project to form the Greater

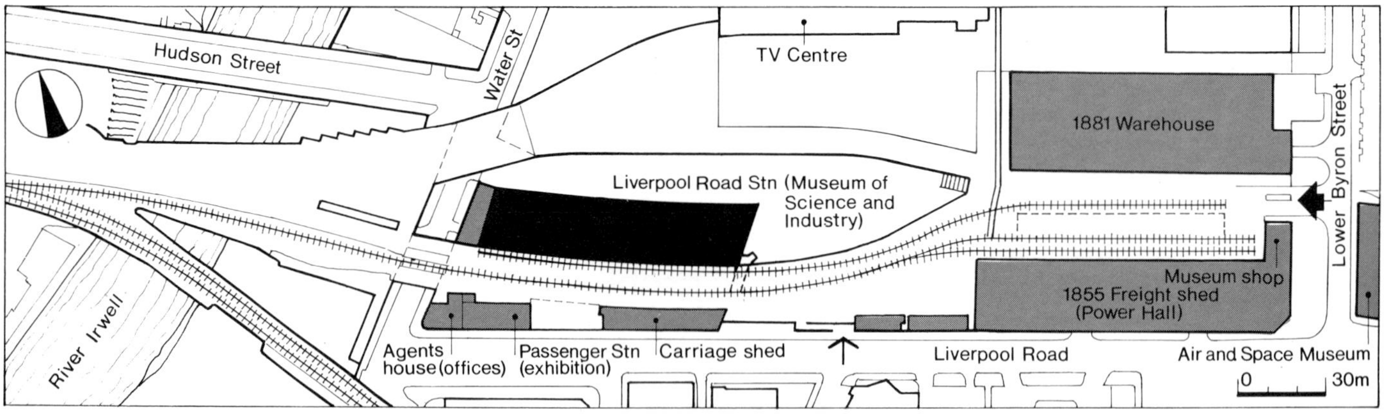

Fig 88 Warehouse, Liverpool Road Station, Manchester: site plan

Fig 89 Warehouse, Liverpool Road Station, Manchester: above, first floor/rail level; below, ground floor/yard level

Manchester Museum of Science and Industry. They hoped that full repair could begin in five years' time and they planned meanwhile to arrest further deterioration and improve the building's appearance. Ventilation and vandalism presented no problems as cross ventilation was naturally good and the site, being railway property, was secure and guarded.

The structure was propped in about 90 places in conjunction with a certain amount of timber treatment. The valleys were newly boarded and a temporary roofing contract with a five year guarantee was placed; this comprised felting the valleys and covering the slates with hessian and bitumen. The treatment was considered suitable

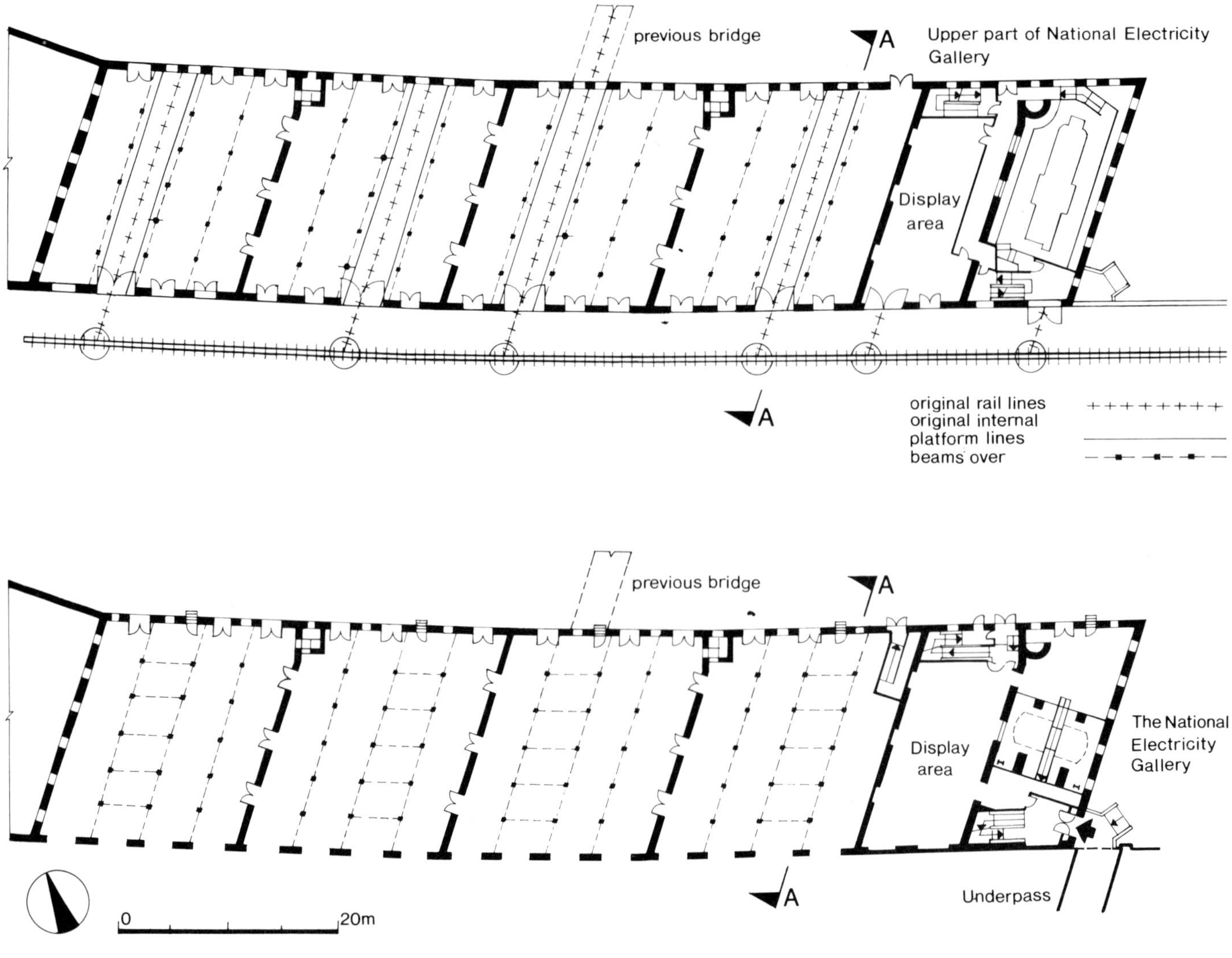

ig 91 Warehouse, Liverpool Road Station, 1anchester: the south side in 1978 before mergency repairs (photo: Greater Manchester ouncil)

ig 92 Warehouse, Liverpool Road Station, 1anchester: after emergency repairs in 1979 the ppearance of the warehouse, and its prospects, vere much improved (photo: A J Pass)

ig 93 Warehouse, Liverpool Road Station, 1anchester: the south side in 1987 seen across 1e rails which are now in use once more for the 1useum of Science and Industry

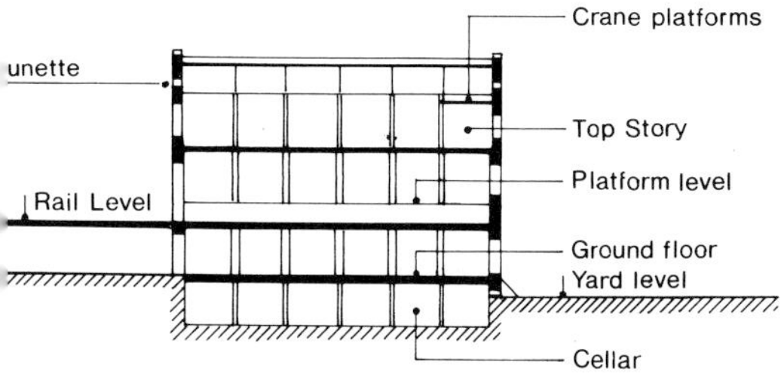

ig 90 Warehouse, Liverpool Road Station, 1anchester: section AA

Fig 94 Warehouse, Liverpool Road Station, Manchester: the first two gables, seen in 1988 from yard level, indicate the east bay which was converted for the National Electricity Gallery in 1984 (photo: English Heritage)

only because the ventilation was good and the slates would, in any case, have to be written off. The gable coping was temporarily patched with brickwork. The most conspicuous elevations were cleaned and repointed. The improved appearance enhanced the building's prospects and brought support from those who had previously failed to appreciate its architectural value. The emergency measures as a whole represented a commitment to full repair in due course.

1983: Beginning of full repair

The first phase of the new museum opened in 1983; in 1984 work was put in hand to establish the National Electricity Gallery in the east bay of the warehouse. This is the bay which was always divided by an extra cross wall and its brick shell has been completely repaired. The nature of the exhibits, including a turbine and generator set from a 1930s power station, involved altering the floor levels and thus removing the historic timber frame.

In 1987 the museum and the Castlefield Urban Heritage Park which surrounds it were already spectacularly successful achievements which appeared to ensure that the rest of the warehouse could be saved intact. The remaining four bays were still untouched, still waiting, and still under emergency repair. They were once more at risk as the five year temporary roofing guarantee had run out and the bituminous treatment was failing, whilst vegetation once more grew behind the parapets. New action was needed to save this magnificent survival with its massive array of timbers and its awesome Piranesian character.

Fig 95 Warehouse, Liverpool Road Station, Manchester: a typical bay of the yard elevation appeared to be once more at risk in 1987

1988: More emergency repairs

Action came in 1988 when a detailed structural survey was followed by the repair of eight local collapses. The roofs and flashings were entirely retreated and the rainwater pipes reconnected; copings were rebedded on the north side. This work was designed to preserve the structure intact for a further five years.

The museum has commissioned a feasibility study which will be used to assist in raising funds for full repair. This time the great timber structure will be respected and it is proposed that the west bay will itself become an exhibit. In conjunction with the passenger station on the other side of the line it will appear as it was in 1830, possibly including trucks on the original rail level.

Fig 96 Warehouse, Liverpool Road Station, Manchester: seven years after emergency repairs the brick and stonework of the railside elevation looked well preserved

Fig 97 Warehouse, Liverpool Road Station, Manchester: the temporary roofing was intended to last five years, but after seven years it was failing

Listing status	Grade II
Local authority	Gateshead Metropolitan Borough Council
Owner for emergency and full repair	Tyne & Wear Metropolitan County Council
Architect	Andrew Brown BA BArch MSc MRTPI, of Tyne & Wear Metropolitan County Council Joint Conservation Team
Cost of emergency repair	£750
Cost of full repair	£7154
Present owner	Tyne & Wear Residuary Body

Case study 8: Brandling Station, Felling, Gateshead

A tiny unwanted building with historic associations

Figs 98–106
This is the original Felling station, built in 1839 for the Brandling Junction Railway which connected South Shields, Gateshead, and Sunderland. A very early passenger station, it stands now without its canopy and platform, a tiny isolated building in a railway cutting bounded by two bridges and high walls.

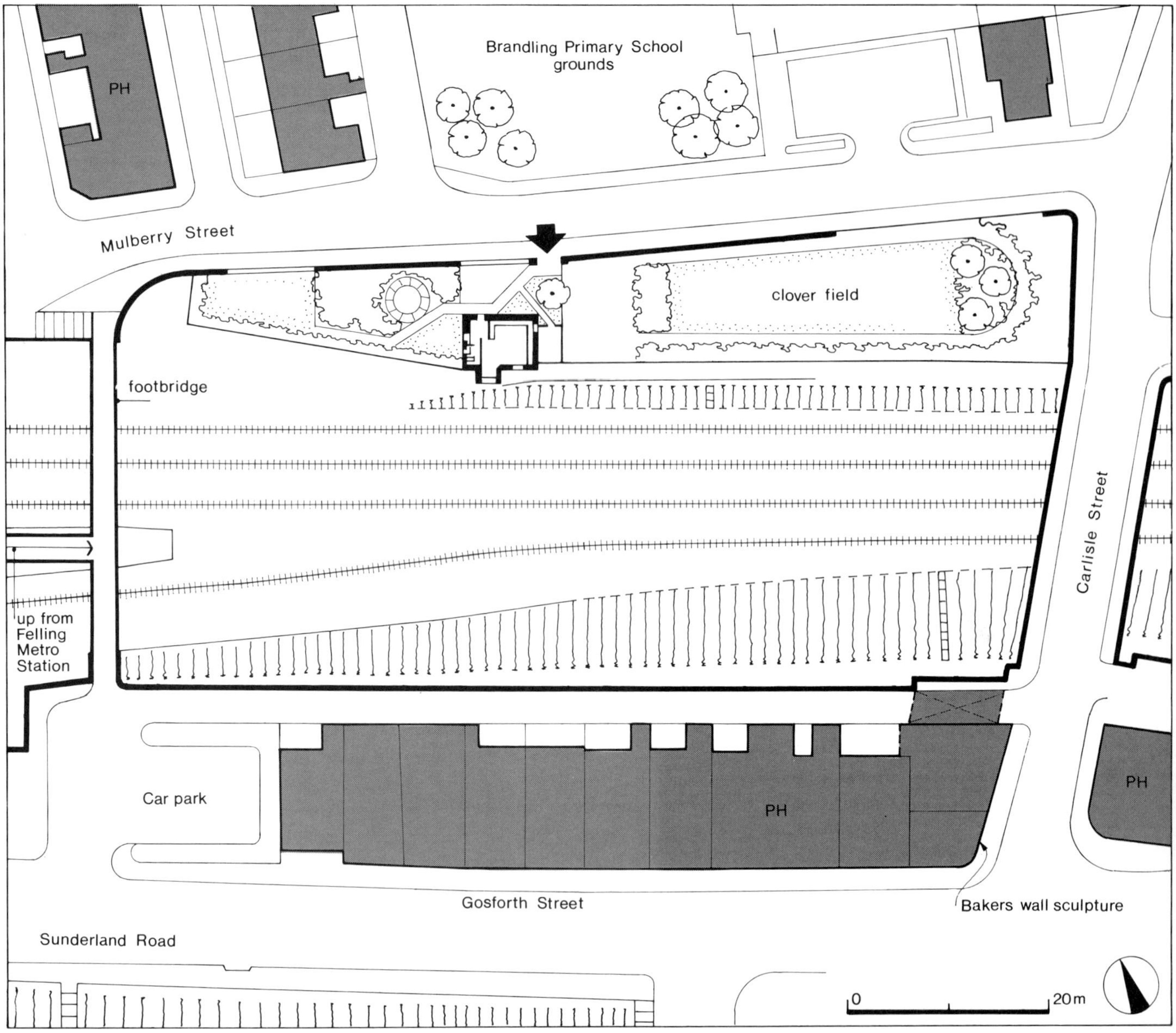

Fig 98 Brandling Station, Felling: ground plan

Fig 99 Brandling Station, Felling, in May 1974 (photo: Tyne & Wear County Council)

Fig 100 Brandling Station, Felling: by October 1974 slates were stolen and copings were being thrown down (photo: Tyne & Wear County Council)

Fig 101 Brandling Station, Felling: temporary roofing and boarding up in 1975 (photo: Tyne & Wear County Council)

Fig 102 Brandling Station, Felling: a neatly sealed window (photo: Tyne & Wear County Council)

It was carefully designed with a three-light Gothic window and steeply pitched gable projecting forward to give a close view of the railway tracks. The slate roofs have two parallel ranges with twin gables at each end and a central gutter. The walls are local sandstone which was also used for gable finials and copings, mullions, dripstones, door arches, and carved plaques. The accommodation cannot have provided more than a waiting room combined presumably with a ticket office.

The causes of decay

The station was closed as early as 1896 and simply left to its fate. During 78 years of disuse the lead was stolen, the roof lost 30–40% of its slates, coping stones were thrown down, and boarded doorways opened up.

1974: Emergency repairs

The newly formed Tyne & Wear Metropolitan County Council had no user in mind but their conservation team perceived the little building in a new light and decided that it must receive at least minimum care. They therefore carried out emergency repairs, refixing slates in some areas and stripping and felting in others. Windows and doors were securely boarded. This work was done by the Gateshead Borough Council's direct labour organisation at the county council's expense and by agreement with British Rail as owners.

1978: Full repair

By 1978 Tyne & Wear County Council had been able to acquire the building together with a strip of land which could be fenced off from the railway track. They sponsored a Manpower Services Commission scheme of full repair. The roof had to be removed and parts of some walls had to be taken down and rebuilt. The intention was to recreate

Fig 104 Brandling Station, Felling, empty but intact in 1987

Fig 103 Brandling Station, Felling: in spite of temporary repairs, the full rehabilitation in 1978 involved demolition of the roof and west gables (photo: Tyne & Wear County Council)

Fig 105 Brandling Station, Felling: the little building is seen by thousands of people passing daily on the Tyne & Wear Metro. In 1987 two of the finials were missing, three were poorly related to the gable copings, and one of these was truncated; the rainwater pipe was missing from the new rainwater head draining the central valley, which was choked with debris

Fig 106 Brandling Station, Felling: the entrance side in 1987 with the side window shuttered and padlocked; beside the entrance door stood the bold and heavy finial which together with its missing partner should have crowned the rear roof

the original external design although this was obviously difficult with the limited skills provided by the MSC.

Internally, a single space was provided for meetings or classes with an entrance lobby and toilet. The strip of land was beautifully laid out to form a miniature landscape and wildlife reserve. The building was then leased by an organisation called 'Town teacher' and used as an urban studies centre for school children.

Ten years later

The staffing for 'Town teacher' was funded by the Manpower Services Commission and was eventually discontinued. The use of the building therefore came to an end in 1985, as did the Tyne & Wear Metropolitan County Council which had brought it back to life. Gateshead Metropolitan Borough Council had no use for it. The Tyne & Wear Residuary Body provided exterior window shutters and a security service, whilst looking for a buyer. Since no sale has taken place, the property is being transferred to Gateshead, who do appreciate its qualities and will continue the search.

Case study 9: The Royal Naval Asylum, Penge, London

Permanent emergency repairs solve a long-standing problem

Listing status	Grade II*
Local authority	London Borough of Bromley
Owner for emergency repair	Greater London Council
Architect for emergency repair	Michael J Stock RIBA MIME, of Greater London Department of Architecture, Historic Buildings Division
Cost of permanent emergency repair	£135,000
Grant for emergency repair	DoE Section 10, £18,500
Leaseholder and contractor for full repair	Fort Knight Construction
Architects for full repair	Ward Associates
Present freeholder	London Borough of Bromley

Figs 107–117

Originally King William IV Naval Foundation, these 12 houses provided free accommodation for widows and orphaned daughters of naval officers. Queen Adelaide founded them in memory of her husband who was known as the sailor king. They were built in 1847 by Philip Hardwick in a Tudor Gothic style using red brickwork with a diaper pattern in grey headers and with Caen stone dressings. The design was elaborate, exaggerating typical almshouse features with many gables and clusters of tall octagonal chimneys. The three groups were unified with horizontal string courses and parapets. The accommodation was generous, providing living room, dining room, and three bedrooms, as well as a tiny maid's bedroom approached by its own winding staircase from the kitchen.

Causes of decay

The houses were occupied from 1848 until 1973 when it had become apparent that very elderly residents were finding it difficult to manage houses of this size. Accordingly the residents were moved to a new scheme in Southwick; the whole group became vacant and was bought by the Greater London Council.

The design of the buildings was the fundamental cause of decay.

Fig 107 The Royal Naval Asylum, Penge: site plan 1848

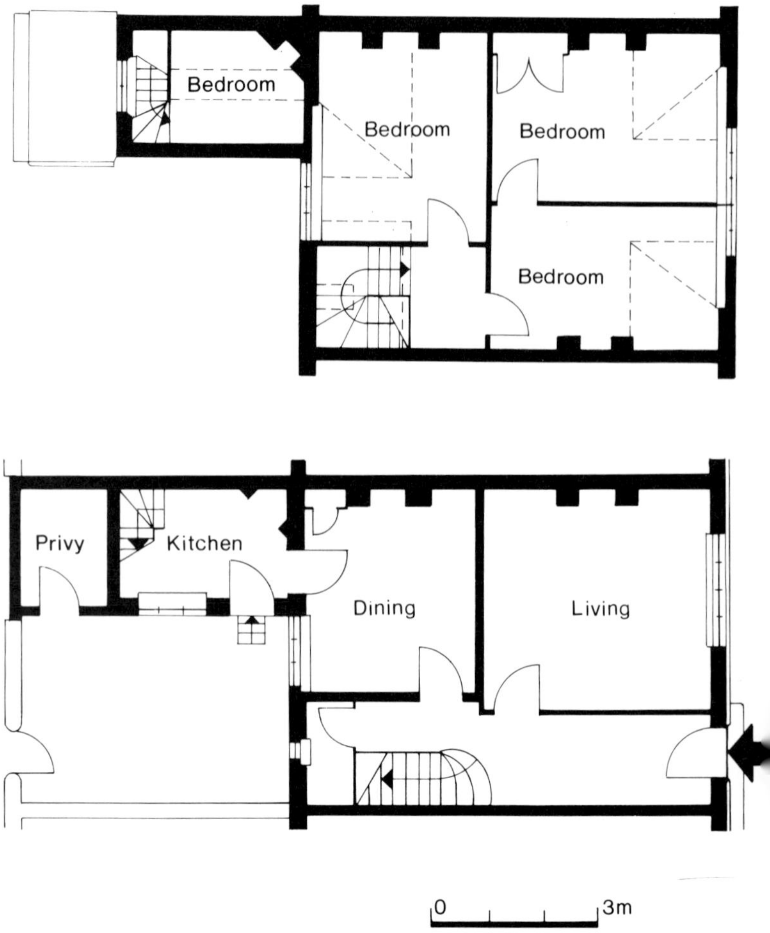

Fig 108 The Royal Naval Asylum, Penge: ground and first floor plans 1848

Fig 109 King William IV Gardens, Penge: site plan 1983

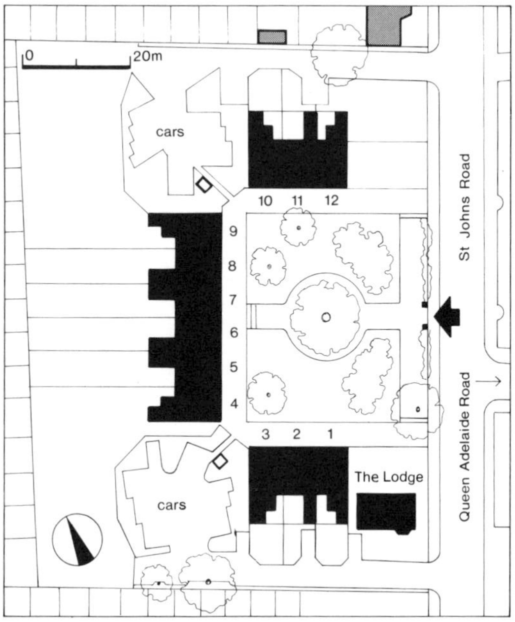

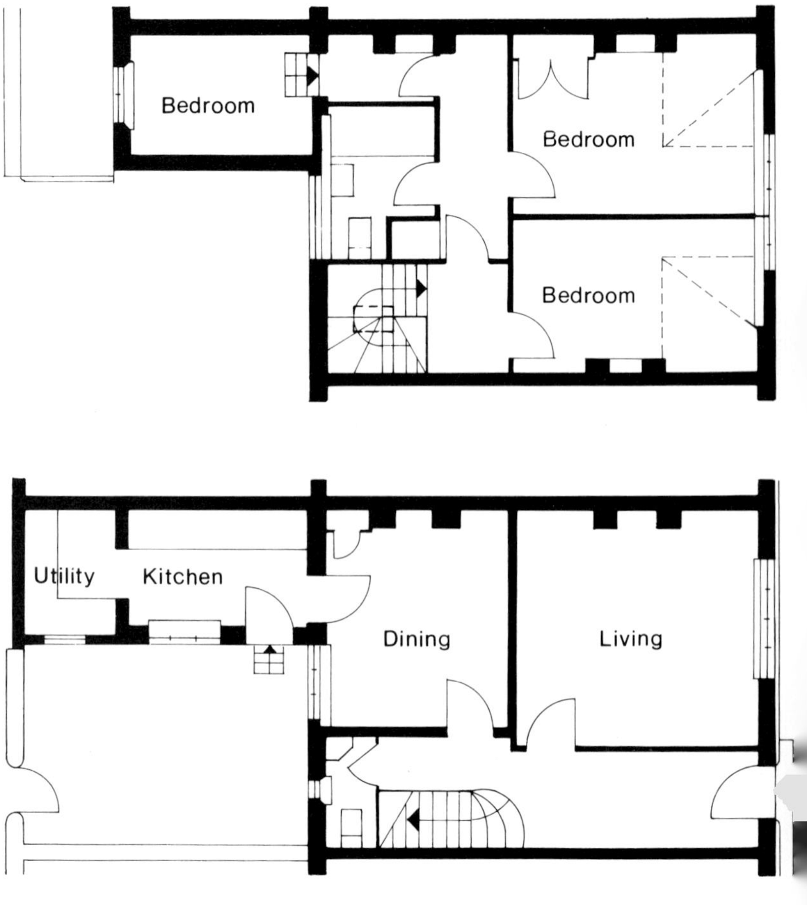

Fig 110 King William IV Gardens, Penge: ground and first floor plans 1983

Philip Hardwick designed the elaborate roofs to discharge water into numerous separate pockets bounded by parapets, with small, and sometimes tortuous, outlets. As the garden trees grew larger, there were more leaves to block the internal gutters. Unseen from the ground, the water built up and penetrated the attics. The chimneys were designed as separate slender octagonal stacks, each cluster joined at the top by a huge brick crown, some of which had begun to separate dangerously.

Fig 111 The Royal Naval Asylum, Penge: the gable of the central block and the linked chimneys of the south block in 1974 (photo: Greater London Photograph Library)

Fig 112 The Royal Naval Asylum, Penge: the back of the north block in 1974 (photo: Greater London Photograph Library)

1974–1980: Emergency repairs

The GLC began to protect the buildings as soon as they were acquired. However, the estimated cost of full repair was so great that neither public nor private sector could produce a viable scheme of modernisation. The GLC therefore carried out permanent emergency

Fig 113 The Royal Naval Asylum, Penge: the rear of number 7 in 1974 showing the complexity of the rainwater disposal system (photo: Greater London Photograph Library)

repairs. They repaired the gables, reslated the roofs with Westmorland slates, overhauled the rainwater system, renewed the flashings, and treated numerous outbreaks of dry rot. The chimneys were repaired by tying the crowns together and strengthening the stacks with reinforced concrete poured from above around new five-inch flue liners.

Fig 114 King William IV Gardens, Penge: the back of the south block in 1987; the compact consistency of Philip Hardwick's design, with yard walls linking rear extensions, is now obscured by fencing to extend the private areas

Fig 115 King William IV Gardens, Penge: the central block in 1987, wholly repaired and completely unchanged; the two rebuilt chimney stacks can be seen on the right

Fig 116 King William IV Gardens, Penge: the original castellated wall links the central and north blocks

In 1980 a further stage of emergency repairs was put in hand. This involved more chimneys, a proportion of the timber casements, and repairs to the Caen stone. More dry rot had to be treated because of lack of maintenance of the rainwater system and thefts of lead between the earlier stages of repair. A 24-hour guard was then instituted but, in spite of this, some more lead was stolen from behind chimney stacks where its absence could not be seen from the ground.

1981–1982: Full repair

The ownership of the buildings was transferred to the London Borough of Bromley which invited tenders for the purchase of a long lease at a peppercorn rent. They stipulated a high standard of renovation, including the rebuilding of two chimney stacks, stone repairs, and the renewal of rainwater heads in the original foliage design. The successful development company, relieved of the great expense of the emergency work, carried out the renovation and sold the houses within a year. The site was divided up into saleable parcels, vehicular access and car parking were provided, and the name was changed to King William IV Gardens. The central landscaped garden was retained.

Five years later

The houses proved to be very popular, in spite of discontent with the developer's actual standard of work and the discovery of extensive untreated dry rot in the ground floors. The value of the 199 year leases has approximately trebled. The historic character and the architectural qualities of the group are much appreciated and the perpetual problem of overhauling the rainwater systems is tackled as a recurring communal event in which all residents participate.

Fig 117 King William IV Gardens, Penge: typical front door and rainwater pipe; the lead pipes were not stolen during the waiting period because the GLC removed them to safe storage

Case study 10: Island Warehouse, Ellesmere Port, Cheshire

Long-term dedication by volunteers

Figs 118–125

The main exhibition space of the National Waterways Museum at Ellesmere Port is the Island Warehouse. This is a two-storey, triple-span grain warehouse built in 1871, with canal basins on three sides, and on the fourth a canal arm running under the first floor structure.

The three gables at each end are powerfully modelled in red and blue bricks with huge stone finials and kneelers. One long elevation is divided into regular recessed bays with loading doors and windows; on the canal arm side the boats can be seen under cover behind a row of 14 free-standing cast iron columns.

The interior with its complete array of cast iron columns and timber caps on both floors has queen trusses and measures about 96×150ft.

The warehouse contributes to an impressive group at the top of the locks combining with the pump house, the accumulator tower, and the Georgian toll house.

Fig 118 Island Warehouse, Ellesmere Port: site plan

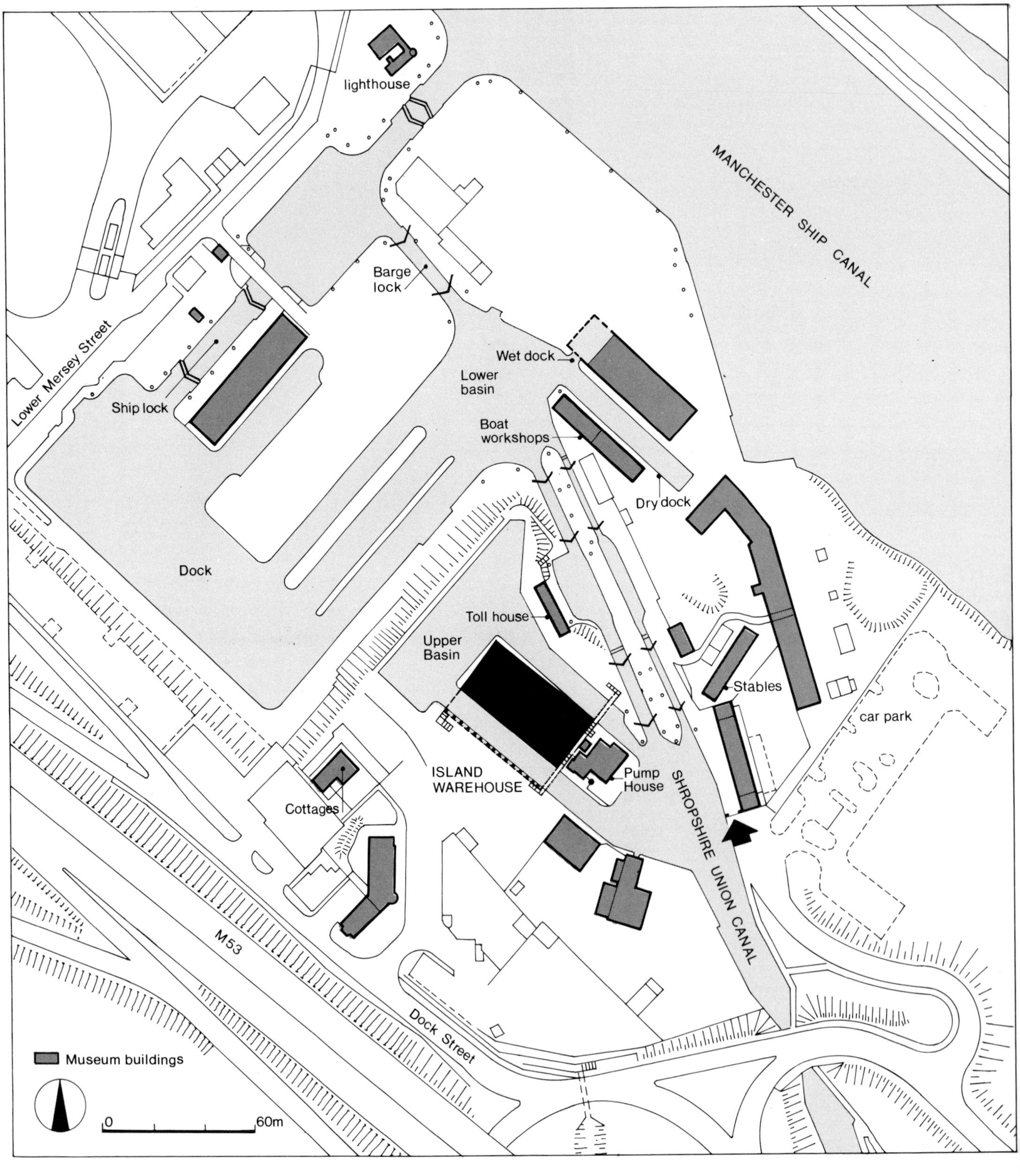

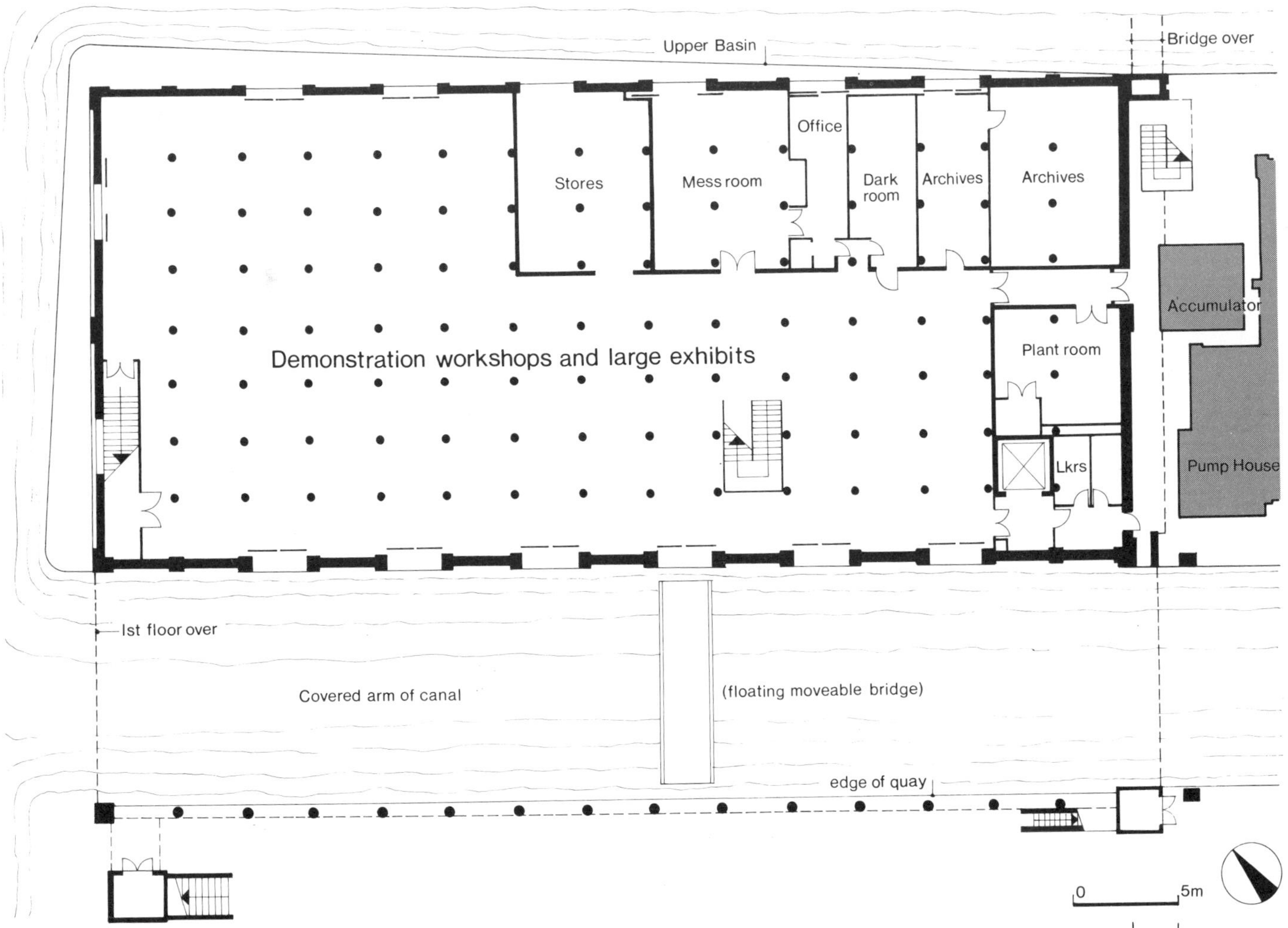

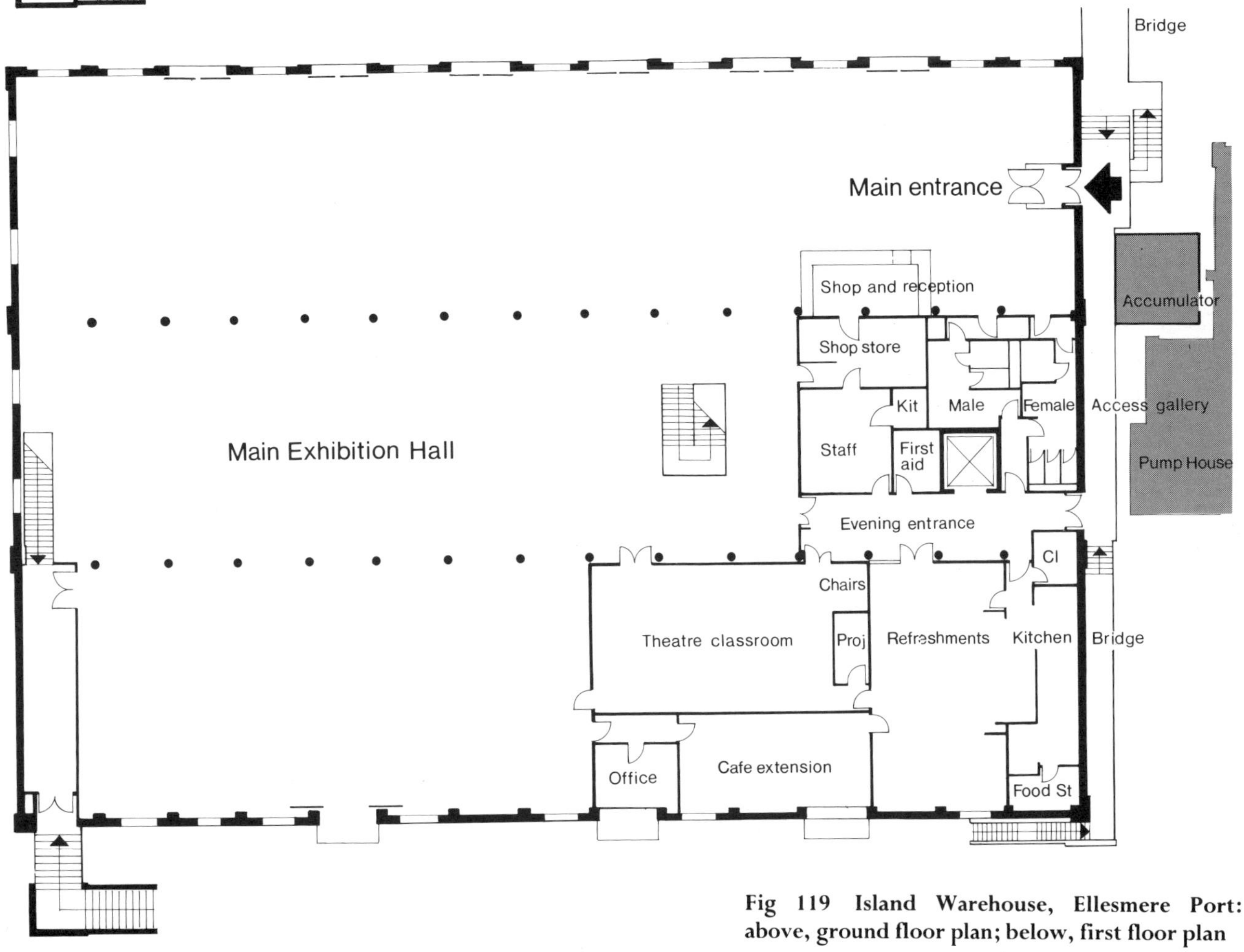

Fig 119 Island Warehouse, Ellesmere Port: above, ground floor plan; below, first floor plan

Fig 120 Island Warehouse, Ellesmere Port: in 1974 the building was open to vandals and the canal arm filled with debris (photo: The Boat Museum Trust)

Fig 121 Island Warehouse, Ellesmere Port: in 1975 clearance was beginning and the windows were boarded; a large and attractive sign declares the future use of the building and that vandals will be prosecuted (photo: The Boat Museum Trust)

The causes of decay

Since the beginning of the nineteenth century the success of Ellesmere Port was mainly due to its use for transhipment of goods between canal boats and larger craft which could sail across the River Mersey or on the high seas. The opening of the Manchester Ship Canal in 1891 brought further importance to the docks, which thus survived well beyond the peak era of the canals. They were still in use after the Second World War and did not finally close until 1958.

During the succeeding 16 years until 1974 no temporary care was provided, and the whole complex group of docks, locks, and historic buildings deteriorated until they were virtually derelict. Vandalism, rain penetration, and fire all took their toll, followed in 1970 by the demolition of Telford's remarkable winged warehouse which dated from 1843. However, the Island Warehouse was one of the buildings to survive, with its floor and roof rotting and its surrounding waterways clogged with rubbish, weed, and demolition materials.

1974–1977: Emergency repairs

In 1974 the new Ellesmere Port and Neston District Council sought a use for this important part of their heritage and agreed with the North Western Museum of Inland Navigation to establish a working boat museum for canal boats and equipment.

Fig 122 Island Warehouse, Ellesmere Port: in 1988 the water was no longer obscured by debris and several museum boats were protected in the canal arm under the warehouse

Fig 123 Island Warehouse, Ellesmere Port: the warehouse from the north in 1988

The immediate task was to prevent further decay on the site, and on the first weekend over 60 museum volunteers came to help block up doors and windows and clear undergrowth. The work continued every weekend with help from local children and teachers. Contrary to predictions the vandalism stopped, partly due to the interest which the local children developed in maintaining the results of their weekends of work, and partly because work progressed continuously every week from then on. Although the huge site was empty on weekdays a guardian presence was established and the ongoing commitment was obvious to the vandals.

Emergency repairs in clearing the interior and the surrounding basins continued during 1975 and 1976. The valley gutters were lined

Fig 124 Island Warehouse, Ellesmere Port: the first floor under conversion to the exhibition area in 1980; the trusses were all taken down and repaired, and rotten timber was replaced and plated at the feet of almost every truss (photo: The Boat Museum Trust)

Listing status	Grade II
Local authority and owner	Ellesmere Port and Neston Borough Council
Users	The Boat Museum Trust Limited
Director since inauguration	Antony Hirst
Cost of emergency repairs	Minimal, see text
Architect for full repair	Architects Department of the Ellesmere Port and Neston Borough Council
Cost of permanent fabric repair	£150,000
Grants for above	DoE Section 10 £20,000; Derelict Land £120,000
Cost of fitting-out contract	£400,000
Grants for above	DoE Section 10 £8000; English Tourist Board £167,000; EEC Regional Fund £158,000; Shell UK £25,000

with felt but this was not successful in protecting the feet of the trusses (when the main repairs were carried out almost all the ends of the trusses had to be replaced). The work cost very little as labour was voluntary, and materials such as concrete blocks and timber were given by the Ship Canal Company and others. It was thus the volunteers themselves who secured the building for the future by their own work.

1978–1982: Full repair

The contract for permanent emergency repair work was finally placed in 1978. This became possible by means of an unprecedented use of Derelict Land grant for the estimated cost of demolition and filling. The volunteers continued to arrive in such numbers and demonstrated such a practical commitment to the site and building that the local authority obtained a £20,000 Section 10 grant from the DoE and topped it up themselves, thus providing the difference between the cost of demolition and basic repair. This enabled the Derelict Land grant to be used for restoration of the Island Warehouse.

The final contract for fitting out the warehouse took place in 1981 and 1982. The fact that money became available for this work from numerous sources was again due to the obvious determination and dedication of the volunteers, who were boat people from the whole canal system of England and Wales.

Five years later

The Boat Museum has become an enormous success with visitor numbers rising to 90,000 per year. Clearing and conservation has extended over the whole site with the help of urban aid money, job creation schemes, Derelict Land grant, and EEC regional aid.

The museum offers permanent and changing exhibitions, a collection of over 50 boats which is still growing, boat restoration, boats in use, an education service, a conference centre, and an ever increasing archive relating to the canal system. Five major museum awards have recently been won, including European Museum of the Year.

Fig 125 Island Warehouse, Ellesmere Port: one of the few original joints where the feet of the trusses remained sound

Listing status	Unlisted
Local authority	Wrekin District Council
Owner	Telford Development Corporation
Architect	W L McMinn, Dip Arch (Oxford) RIBA, of the Severn Gorge Project Team, Telford Development Corporation
Emergency repair carried out by	Telford Development Corporation from their land and properties budget
First tenants	Ironbridge Gorge Museum Trust and the Manpower Services Commission
Cost of materials for first stage of full repair	Approx £220,000
Present tenants	Maw's Craft Centre

Case study 11: Maw's Tileworks, Ironbridge, Shropshire

Irreparable damage in one year of neglect

Figs 126–134

The present impressive ranges of buildings are all that remain of Maw's Benthall Works at Jackfield, built in 1883 by Charles Lynam, and once the largest decorative tile factory in the world.

Two- and three-storey warehouses face each other across a tapering courtyard and are linked at one end by an office building spanning the main entrance. The office building has a fine staircase but only the remnants are left of the once magnificent tiling and the superb memorial plaque which decorated the walls. There are directors' offices with bay windows, drawing offices, and administration spaces, all with fine but functional pine joinery. The brick warehouses have cast iron internal columns, timber first floors, and a complete array of massive king post roof trusses. The group is punctuated by a four-storey millhouse which has an external hoist surmounted by a canopy.

The factory made architectural faience, encaustic floor tiles, reproductions of medieval tiles, glazed high relief wall tiles, mosaics,

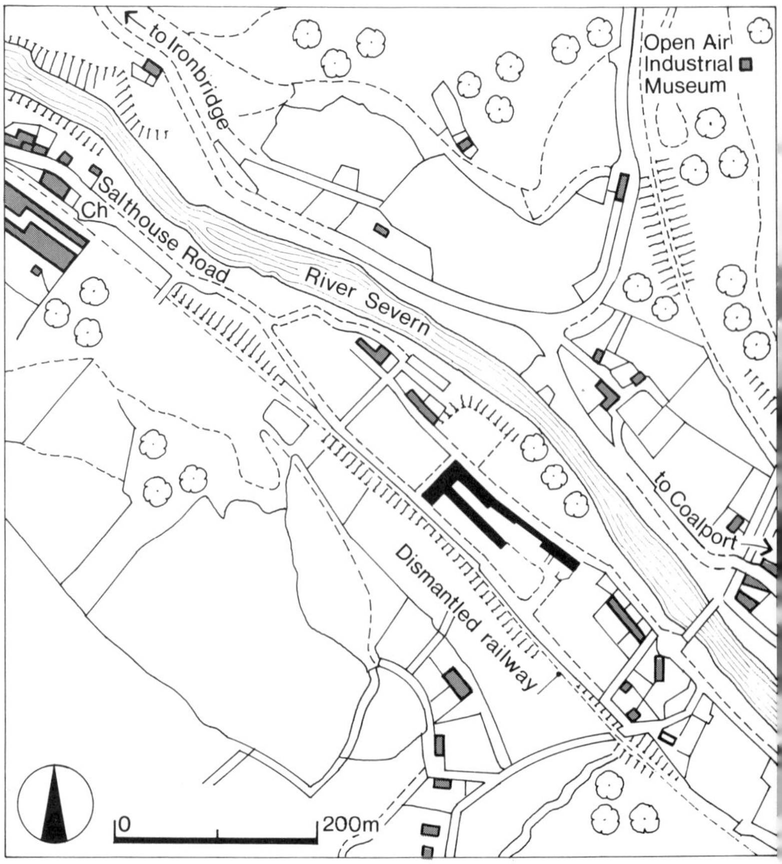

Fig 126 Maw's Tileworks, Ironbridge: location plan

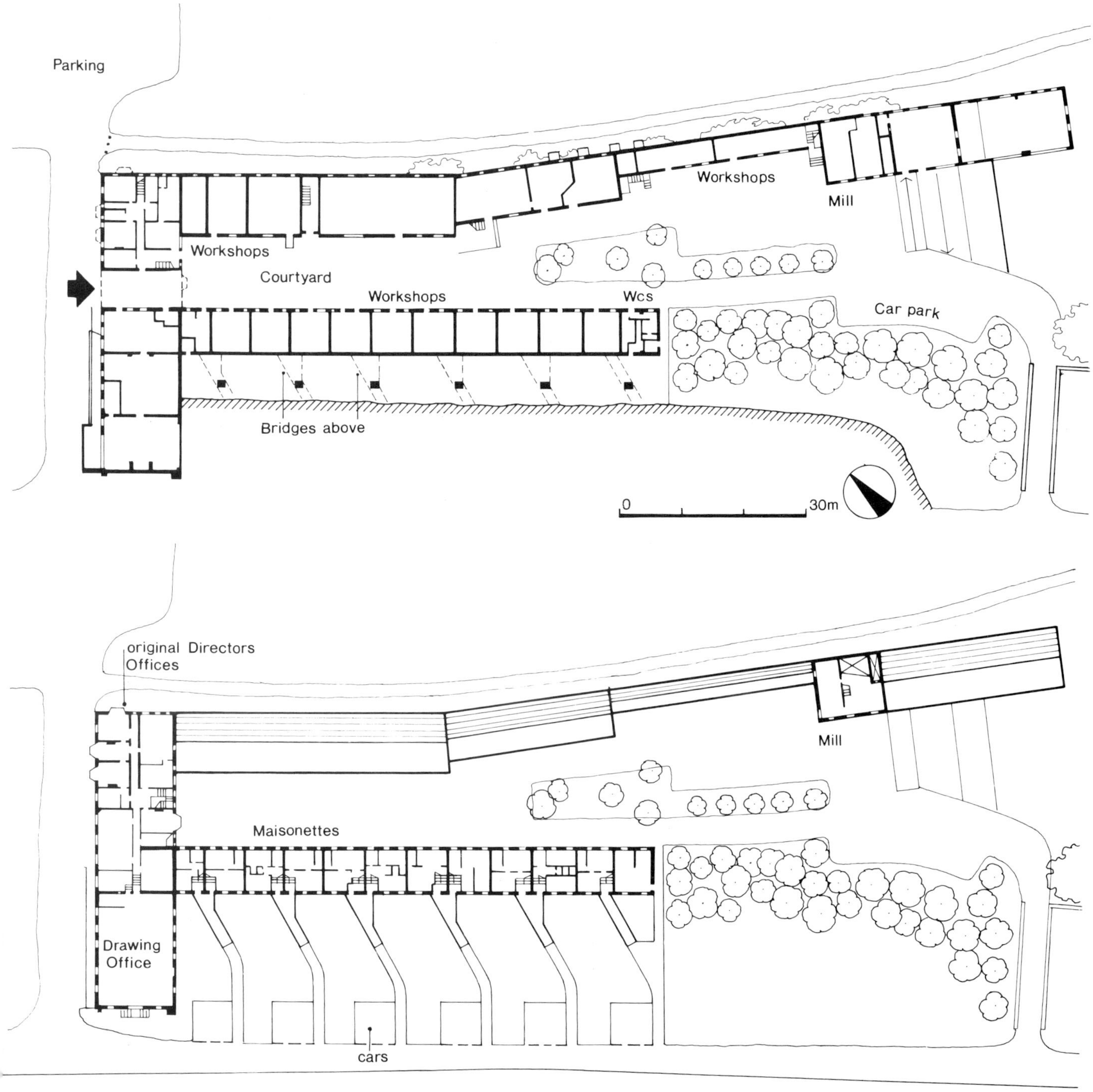

Fig 127 Maw's Tileworks, Ironbridge: above, ground floor plan; below, first floor plan

glazed tiles decorated with transfer prints, and complete pictorial and decorative panels for wall and floors. These tiles can be seen in houses, churches, pubs, and shops all over the country and were exported worldwide. As fashions changed in the twentieth century the designs changed too, encompassing art nouveau, art deco, and silk screen prints. In the 1920s and 1930s considerable quantities of plain tiles with friezes were made for kitchens and bathrooms, and mottled tiles for fireplaces.

The causes of decay

Demand dwindled steadily after the Second World War when more and more work was specified in plain tiles. Finally, a series of

Fig 128 Maw's Tileworks, Ironbridge: the Mill building in 1973 closely surrounded by unwanted buildings (photo: A T Herbert)

takeovers submerged the company in the gigantic H & R Johnson-Richards Tiles, based in Stoke, and production ceased at Jackfield in 1969.

The whole vast complex of buildings was becoming thoroughly run down by that time and when it became empty no thought was given to its protection. In a single year the staircase tiling was stolen and virtually all the windows were broken; skylights rotted and extensive dry rot became apparent in the office building and the adjoining workshops.

1970–1978: Emergency repairs

Recognising the heritage value of the buildings, Telford Development Corporation bought the whole group and began the protection of

Fig 129 Maw's Tileworks, Ironbridge: the courtyard in 1973; the subsequent removal of the central buildings revealed a potentially attractive environment (photo: A T Herbert)

the fabric. Rotten skylights were removed and replaced by patch repairs of roof tiles. The building was secured against vandals by nailing plain galvanised iron sheeting to the outsides of all the lower windows, using galvanised clout nails at about 100mm centres. This was very strong indeed, especially as the sheeting was backed all over by small-pane wood window frames. It kept the vandals out but inevitably caused some damage to the windows. It totally blocked the ventilation and thus made it more difficult to arrest the dry rot.

An important contribution to the emergency repairs was the scheme of selective demolition. The vast majority of factory buildings were removed, thus improving the chances of survival for those which remained. At the same time a farsighted plan of extensive land shaping and planting was put into effect. An enormous riverside waste tip was removed and the material taken round to the south side to fill the site of the demolished tunnel kiln. The remaining buildings now stand in a woodland setting between the dismantled railway and the River Severn, which were their original lifelines.

The second stage of emergency repairs began in 1977 when the Development Corporation backed the Ironbridge Gorge Museum Trust in the conception of creating a tile museum alongside a training

Fig 130 Maw's Tileworks, Ironbridge: the huge 'biscuit' warehouse under emergency repair in 1979 with the windows well protected; the galvanised sheeting was never penetrated and lasted here for twelve years; in some unused parts of the complex the sheeting is still in place after 17 years (photo: A T Herbert)

Fig 131 Maw's Tileworks, Ironbridge: the top floor of the 'biscuit' warehouse in 1973, formerly used for the mosaic department; the building was strengthened in 1982 by building crosswalls to form individual dwellings and workshops (photo: A T Herbert)

workshop; the workshop reproduced the old tiles for restoration work and undertook new commissions for decorative tiles of all kinds.

Unemployment was, and still is, very severe in Telford and funds extremely difficult to find for museum work. However, continuous work was established with Manpower Services Commission schemes, thus assuring the use of one of the warehouses and the surveillance of the rest of the group. The training workshop was established with 40 places for the Youth Opportunities Programme. A Community Enterprise Programme was used for the repair of the buildings. All these schemes depended utterly on the skill of the supervisors who needed to combine the qualities of youth leaders, organisers, and craftsmen. Without these skills, and without the special labour schemes, this group of buildings would have been lost.

The third stage of emergency repairs in the early 1980s included permanent work to the office building. The timberwork of the bay windows was completely renewed; the roof and bell tower were repaired; the original main entrance and iron gates leading into the courtyard were repaired and painted; the windows were repaired and glazed, thus letting light into the interior. This work has helped to give the whole group a more promising appearance and highlighted

Fig 132 Maw's Tileworks, Ironbridge: the Manpower Services Commission team in 1979 standing at the entrance gateway below the office building (photo: A T Herbert)

the unusual character of the architecture. The major work of restoring the interior of the office building and putting it to use is still to come.

1982–1985: The first stage of full repair

During this period the Telford Development Corporation sponsored Manpower Services Commission schemes to repair fully the huge 'biscuit' warehouse where partly-fired tiles used to be stored. This is the southern arm of the group and comprised an enormous

Fig 133 Maw's Tileworks, Ironbridge: the office building under emergency repair (photo: A T Herbert)

undivided area measuring 75×7m and three floors high. The road behind is one and a half floors above the courtyard, because of the steep slope of the site down to the Severn Gorge.

The scheme has created 11 split level dwellings of varying sizes in the upper floors. These are entered from the road by a series of bridges. At courtyard level are 11 craft workshops which, together with nine on the other side of the courtyard, now comprise Maw's Craft Centre. All the dwellings and almost all the workshops are occupied by a variety of craftworkers including a potter, a tile maker, and a tile conservator. The museum activities have moved to what is now the Ironbridge Gorge Museum Trust's Jackfield Tile Museum in the old Craven Dunhill factory just to the north.

1988: The future of the group

The management committee of the Craft Centre has formed a private limited company which is buying the buildings from Telford Development Corporation. They propose to restore the unused buildings and expand the present activities. The most intractable but most interesting of the remaining rehabilitation projects will be the office building and the four-storey mill building.

The mill is still at risk, no longer from vandals but from the weather; the exposed timber work of the hoist is especially

Fig 134 Maw's Tileworks, Ironbridge: the courtyard in 1987; the 'biscuit' warehouse on the left was in full use as workshops with dwellings above; the office building at the end had received permanent repairs to the outside only; the mill building on the right was deteriorating and at risk

vulnerable. The original galvanised sheets are still effective in the lower windows but the polythene protection to the upper windows has become degraded and torn and now admits rain and birds. The pointing has been washed out of the large buttresses on the lower side and the sloping surfaces support a vigorous growth of vegetation. This is a difficult building with very low beam heights, but it makes an immense architectural contribution to the group.

Proposals so far put forward for these buildings have included converting the mill into four flats and using the office building to further the interests of the Craft Centre. Suggested uses have been showrooms, teaching areas, shared office services, and areas for demonstrations and exhibitions.

Case study 12: 32 Heathcoat Street, Nottingham

Permanent emergency repairs to a valuable street elevation

Figs 135–140

This building was the Spanish Consulate, built in 1883 by Charles Vernon Taylor on the edge of Nottingham's Lace Market. It has three storeys surmounted by a dormer and a gable, all of very fine and elaborately detailed red brickwork. The design is striking and original, and, although the street frontage presents an uninterrupted line of late nineteenth-century buildings, this one stands out as something special.

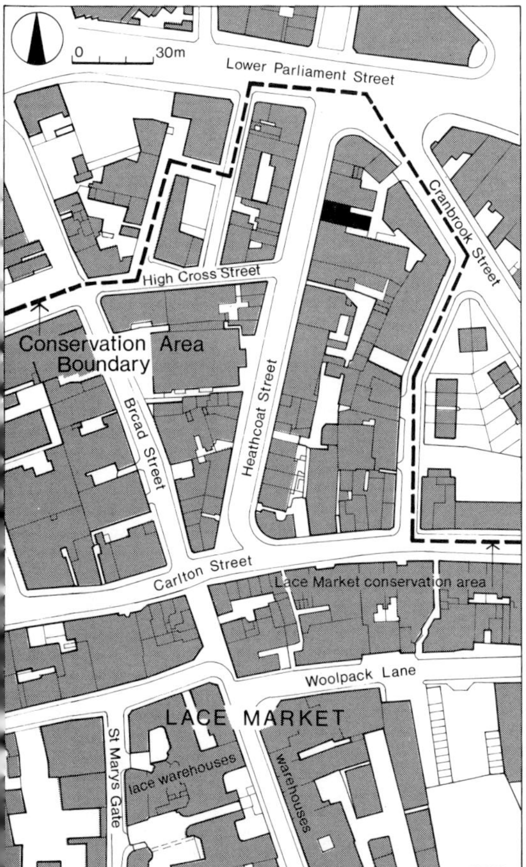

Fig 135 32 Heathcoat Street, Nottingham: location plan

The causes of decay

The building had been bought by the City Council when it was anticipated that a major road scheme (Sherriff's Way) along the eastern side of the Lace Market would involve the demolition of many properties in the area. The scheme was subsequently abandoned and the building was put to various uses, including a hostel for the homeless. During this period it was damaged by fire and in 1973 it was left empty.

Gradually the building became badly affected by dry rot; it reached a critical state of disrepair and no tenant could be found. The Council gave active consideration to demolition but was persuaded to continue to advertise the premises either for sale or to let at a nominal sum.

1978: Emergency repairs

It was estimated that full repair would cost £46,000 but this sum was not available. Limited work was therefore undertaken by the Council and the Nottinghamshire Building Preservation Trust to

Listing status	Local interest
Local authority and owner	Nottingham City Council
Architect	Nottingham City Council Technical Services and Planning Department
Cost of emergency repair	£2800
Grants for emergency repair	DoE (non-outstanding conservation areas) £1400; Nottinghamshire Building Preservation Trust £1300
Cost of full repair	£58,000

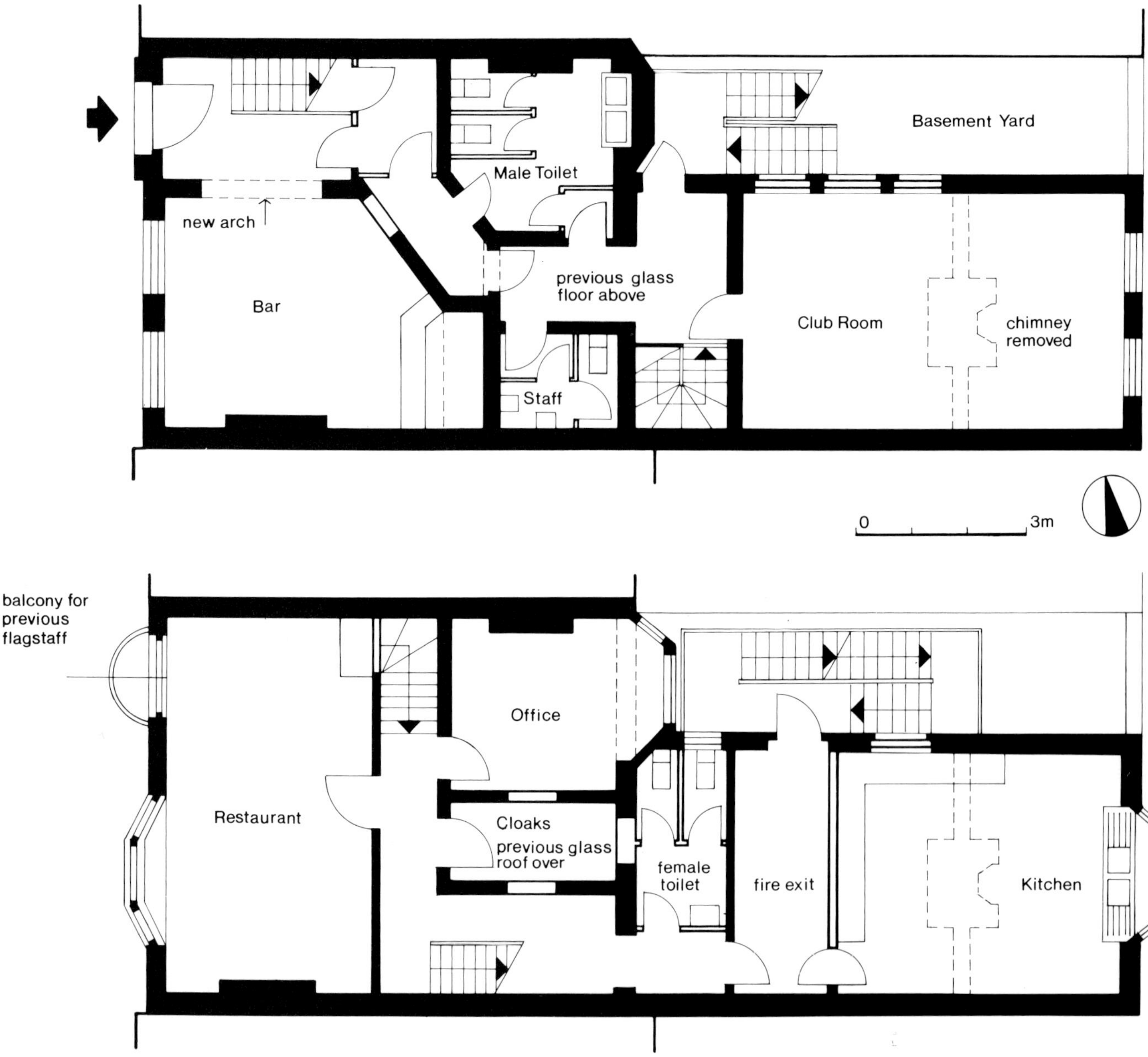

Fig 136 32 Heathcoat Street, Nottingham: above, ground floor plan; below, first floor plan

safeguard the structure and make the property more attractive to buyers or lessees.

The work included eradication of dry rot, replacement of rainwater goods, and repairs to the roof and staircase. The front elevation was carefully cleaned, revealing the details of the brickwork. Decaying joinery in the bay window and the front door frame was replaced, and all the woodwork on this elevation was repainted. The windows were not boarded up, but the sashes were infilled with a matt black, vandal-resistant sheet material instead of glass.

This limited but mainly permanent work to the facade showed up its fine qualities and made a dramatic impact on the street scene. As a result interest was shown in the building.

Fig 137 32 Heathcoat Street, Nottingham, before emergency repair; with its fine brickwork concealed by 95 years of grime it blended into a drab streetscape and offered no appeal to prospective users (photo: Nottingham City Council Planning Department)

Fig 138 32 Heathcoat Street, Nottingham, after emergency repair in 1978; the brickwork was conspicuously attractive, the joinery repaired and painted, and the windows infilled with sheet material instead of glass (photo: Nottingham City Council Planning Department)

Fig 139 32 Heathcoat Street, Nottingham, in 1988 (photo: English Heritage)

Fig 140 32 Heathcoat Street, Nottingham: a detail showing the fine quality of the brickwork in 1987

1980: Full repair

Within two years the building was successfully let and fully renovated for use as a social club.

Eight years later

There was a change of use in 1985 from a club to a restaurant; this use lapsed and the building was once more on the market to be let or sold. In 1988 it was leased to the Nottingham Counselling Centre.

The building is now within the Lace Market conservation area and its fortunes have a good chance of rising with the fast-growing interest in this important part of Nottingham.

5 Aspects of the case studies

5.1 Choice of buildings

The common thread running through these 12 studies is that of buildings of historic interest which have suffered perilous decline into disrepair and sometimes into near dereliction. They all survive, not all with obviously brilliant futures, but all with better prospects and some with spectacular success.

The buildings were chosen in 1978 and 1981 after enquiries to conservation officers and others all over England. The aim was to find a variety of buildings where there was a record of emergency repairs having been carried out. It was difficult to identify such buildings and the resulting 12 are thus a random sample and do not yield information for soundly based conclusions. Nevertheless it is interesting to consider in these cases what measures were taken, or could have been taken, to arrest the initial decline, what the emergency repairs cost, whether they were well done, and what they achieved. Table 1 shows the bare facts with approximate dates and figures as far as these are known.

5.2 First steps

It is not very constructive to state that the emergency repairs would have been more effective if carried out sooner; however, it may be useful to ask whether advance preparations for vacancy could have preempted the need for emergency repairs.

In the cases of the Lamb Inn, Elder Street, Arkwright House, and the Cheltenham houses important listed buildings were vacated by owners between 1955 and 1977; it is worth considering now whether current conservation teams would have enough foreknowledge to encourage, or even ensure, proper preparations in similar circumstances. The properties in Gillygate and Heathcoat Street were bought to be demolished for road schemes between 1950 and 1973. It is by now abundantly clear that these schemes take many years to come to fruition, are frequently shelved or altered, and that until the day of demolition actually arrives a listed building should be cared for. Preparations for an unknown future could have been made for the Island Warehouse in 1958 and for Maw's Tileworks in 1969, but neither of these buildings was listed and they were abandoned unprotected by their departing owners; action by both local authorities, although fairly swift in the case of the tileworks, did not come until some irreparable damage had taken place.

Two buildings out of the 12 did receive timely action. The Greater Manchester Council carried out temporary repairs to the Liverpool Road warehouse even before they bought it from British Rail; the Greater London Council bought the Royal Naval Asylum when it became empty and carried out permanent protective repairs to tide it over the waiting period.

5.3 The cost of emergency repairs

It would be interesting to compare the cost of emergency repairs with the ultimate cost of full repair. These figures are not available but in some cases the emergency repairs can be considered, with hindsight, as a percentage of full rehabilitation. Table 1 indicates that in five cases, all relating to temporary repairs, the percentages were very low, varying from negligible sums to 2.6%

For Elder Street and Brandling Station the work included a degree of permanent repair and the percentage rises to 8% and 10% respectively.

The largest sums of money were spent on the Liverpool Road warehouse and the Royal Naval Asylum, the first because of its size and the second because the repairs were permanent.

5.4 The quality of the emergency repairs

Chapter 2 of this book describes a policy of minimum care for historic buildings when nothing else is possible. Against this yardstick the emergency repairs to the Elder Street houses and to the Liverpool Road warehouse were very good. The results were very different because of the time factor. In Elder Street it was correctly forecast that full repair would be completed within a year; in Manchester a period of five years was estimated and ten years passed, with a change of ownership and a lack of continuing care before new action was taken.

For Arkwright House very short-term first aid repairs were well carried out. The Royal Naval Asylum and Heathcoat Street demonstrate that high quality permanent repairs, even if limited in scope, should always be the preferred policy.

The emergency work to the Lamb Inn and to the Cheltenham houses fell far short of minimum care.

At Maw's Tileworks the very high cost of temporary repairs to a huge group of unlisted historic buildings was mitigated by selective demolition; the prospects for the remaining buildings were then enhanced by permanent landscaping.

5.5 Achievements

In every case the emergency repairs demonstrated a commitment to the building which ensured its survival. It seems, therefore, that very small sums can achieve this primary success, especially when dedicated people are involved. Amongst these people were an entrepreneurial group, an historic buildings trust, a body specially constituted to befriend the building, bands of volunteers with the enthusiasm actually to carry out the work, determined local authorities, several conservation teams, and three museum groups.

Those repairs coming in the lower categories of expenditure did not actually achieve very much in the way of saving historic items at risk. Typically, the work did prevent cumulative decay although the items which it should have saved were frequently replaced during the main rehabilitation contract. The degree of success could perhaps be measured by the extent to which historic features were ultimately retained in their original form. For example, the emergency repairs were very well and meticulously carried out for the Elder Street houses with great success; on the other hand the Cheltenham houses retain virtually nothing of the original features, the Regency elevation having been carefully recreated.

The permanent repairs clearly achieved a saving of money on the full rehabilitation contract. The temporary repairs cannot be shown to have done the same, but proper minimum care, applied before substantial deterioration set in, would save money in the long term.

It could be asked whether the whole protracted procedure, lasting in these 12 cases between 2 and 82 years, was worthwhile. The answer is that the waiting period is generally very short in relation to the life of the building and that if the building is worth listing it must be worth minimum care. Finally no one could visit the Lamb Inn, Elder Street, Gillygate, Rock Hall, the Royal Naval Asylum, or the Island Warehouse without being struck by the brilliant success of the rehabilitation in architectural and in human terms. As for the buildings whose future is still uncertain, what are a few years in the life of an historic building and does it not deserve at least minimum care while waiting?

Table 1 Case studies

Case study	*Title*	*Year built*	*Year vacated*	*Rehabilitation complete*	*Years of waiting*	*Cost of emergency repairs £*	*% cost**
1	The Lamb Inn, Wallingford	1505	1960	1979	19	5200	2.6
2	5–7 Elder Street, Spitalfields	1726	1977	1979	2	6500	8.3
3	Arkwright House, Preston	1728	1953	1980	27	100	0.04
4	Gillygate, York	C19 & C18	1950–65	1978–87	*c* 25	15,500	
5	Rock Hall, Farnworth	1820	1976	1981	5	2500	1.9
6	113–115 Bath Road, Cheltenham	1825	1972	1979	7	1580	1.6
7	Liverpool Road Warehouse, Manchester	1830	1976			60,000	
8	Brandling Station, Felling	1839	1896	1978	82	750	10
9	Royal Naval Asylum, Penge	1847	1973	1982	9	135,000	
10	Island Warehouse, Ellesmere Port	1871	1958	1982	24	300	0.2
11	Maw's Tileworks, Ironbridge	1883	1969				
12	32 Heathcoat Street, Nottingham	1883	1973	1980	7	2800	4.8

*emergency repair cost as an approximate percentage of full rehabilitation where known

Appendix

1 (section 1.9) Architectural Heritage Fund, 17 Carlton House Terrace, London SW1Y 5AW, telephone 01-925 0199.

2 (section 2.4.1) For crack monitoring equipment send for catalogue showing discs and gauges from Avongard Ltd, Down Road, Portishead, Bristol BS2D 8RB, telephone 0272 849782.

3 (section 2.4.1) For firms to carry out support scaffolding obtain recommendations from the National Association of Scaffolding Contractors, 82 New Cavendish Street, London W1M 8AD, telephone 01-580 5588.

4 (section 2.5.2) Amenity societies can be contacted through the local planning officer. Addresses of secretaries of registered societies can also be obtained from the Civic Trust, 17 Carlton House Terrace, London SW1Y 5AW, telephone 01-930 0914.

5 (section 2.5.4(B)) Reusable security door screens are obtainable from Armadillo Products Ltd, Trent Lane, Nottingham NG2 4DS, telephone 0602 587064, and from Sitex Security Products Ltd, Polygon House, 18–20 Bromells Road, London SW4 0BG, telephone 01-622 9400.

6 (section 2.5.4(E)) For anti-climbing paint obtain names of products and makers from the Paint Research Association, 8 Waldegrave Road, Teddington, Middlesex TW11 8LD, telephone 01-977 4427. Typical products are obtainable from Camrex Ltd, Industrial Division, PO Box 34, Washington, Tyne & Wear NE37 1QJ, telephone 091-417 7000, and from J W Bollom and Company Ltd, PO Box 78, Croydon Road, Elmers End, Beckenham, Kent BR3 4BL, telephone 01-658 2299.

7 (section 2.5.4(E)) Make up a spiked collar as illustrated or obtain equivalent galvanised 'Anti-Scaling Barrier Pipe Guard Unit', either wall-mounted or pipe-mounted, from the Expanded Metal Company Ltd, PO Box 14, Longhill Industrial Estate (North), Hartlepool TS25 1PR, telephone 0429 266633.

8 (section 2.5.5) Closed metal letter containers can be obtained from J B Architectural Ironmongery Ltd, Avis Way, Newhaven, East Sussex BN9 0GU, telephone 0273 514961, from The Safety Letter Box Company Ltd, Unit 5, Millands Industrial Park, Milland Road, Neath, West Glamorgan SA11 1NJ, telephone 0639 53525, and from builders merchants such as Nicholls and Clarke Ltd, 3–10 Shoreditch High Street, London E1 6PE, telephone 01-247 5432.

9 (section 2.5.6) National Supervisory Council for Intruder Alarms, Queensgate House, 14 Cookham Road, Maidenhead, Berkshire SL6 8AJ, telephone 0628 37512.

10 (section 2.5.7) Names of makers of anti-graffiti barrier treatments can be obtained from the address of the Paint Research Association given in Appendix entry 6 above.

11 (section 2.6.1(A)) Advice should be obtained direct from the makers whose telephone numbers can be obtained from the Association of British Roofing Felt Manufacturers Ltd, 69 Cannon Street, London EC4N 5AB, telephone 01-248 4444. A suitable material would be about 180g/m^2 and about 29kg/roll, such as Permanite Hyperoof 180 sanded finish.

12 (section 2.6.1(A)) Sylglas standard mastic tape is made by Winn and Coales (Denso) Ltd, Denso House, Chapel Road, West Norwood, London SE27 0TR, telephone 01-670 7511.

13 (section 2.6.1(C)) For repair of asphalt roofs use, for example, Febflex Bitumen mastic and Febflex scrim bedded in and covered with Febflex roofing compound, all from Feb (Great Britain) Ltd, Albany House, Swinton Hall Road, Swinton, Manchester M27 1DT, telephone 061-794 7411. Another typical series of products is Aquaseal 88 mastic, Aquaseal reinforcing fabric, and Aquaseal 40 waterproofing, all from Aquaseal Ltd, Kingsnorth Hoo, Rochester, Kent ME3 9ND, telephone 0634 250722.

14 (section 2.6.1(D)) Patch repairs to felt roofing with a 'torch on' material can only be carried out by experienced roofing contractors; because of the fire risk the work should not be attempted under overhanging eaves or in similar high risk areas. The maker of the material will advise on a suitable weight for the particular application but the lightest weight should probably be chosen for a temporary repair unless the failure is due to structural movement. Where the fire risk precludes the use of heat, cold applied liquids may have to be used such as Ruberoid Ruberflex together with the accompanying cleaner and primer. Technical advice for a particular situation can be obtained from The Flat Roofing Contractors' Advisory Board, Maxwelton House, 41–43 Boltro Road, Haywards Heath, West Sussex RH16 1BJ, telephone 0444 440027. Technical advice on products and procedures should be obtained from the makers, as in Appendix entry 11 above.

15 (section 2.6.2) Sylglas standard mastic tape as in Appendix entry 12 above.

16 (section 2.6.4) Ventilators fitting into brick perpends are made by Ryton's Building Products Ltd, 58–60 Roundhill Road, Kettering, Northants NN15 6BG, telephone 0536 511874.

17 (section 2.6.4) Plastic ventilators which can be inserted into a roof slope to replace three plain tiles are made by Redland Roof Tiles Ltd, Reigate, Surrey RH2 0SJ, telephone 0737 242488, and by Steetley Brick and Tile Ltd, Roofing Division, Ridge Hill Drive, Madeley Heath, Crewe, Cheshire CW3 9LY, telephone 0782 750243. Concrete ventilation roof tiles for plain tiling are made by The Marley Roof Tile Company Ltd, 1 Suffolk Way, Sevenoaks, Kent TN13 1YL, telephone 0732 741500. 'Zamba' aluminium ventilators for slate roofs are made by Nicholl and Wood Ltd, Netherton Works, Holmfield, Halifax, West Yorkshire HX3 6ST, telephone 0422 244484.

18 (section 2.6.4) Wire netting in a chimney pot can be adapted by birds to form a nesting site, and in this case a permanent remedy would be an inserted 'weatherguard top' made in four sizes and three colours by Red Bank Manufacturing Company Ltd, Measham, Burton-on-Trent, Staffordshire DE12 7EL, telephone 0530 70333.

19 (section 2.6.5) For firms experienced in scaffolding and sheeting consult the National Association of Scaffolding Contractors at the address given in Appendix entry 3 above.

20 (section 2.6.7) For frost protection of indoor installations the recommended insulation thicknesses are as in BS 6700 and depend upon the pipe diameter and the thermal conductivity of the insulating material. Typical products for pipe sizes with nominal outside diameters up to 42mm would be Armstrong AF Armaflex of 22mm wall thickness, Pilkingtons Crown Pipe Insulation of 25mm wall thickness, or Rocksil Pipe Insulation of 32mm wall thickness.

21 (section 2.7.2) For information on identification and treatment of woodboring insects see *Building Research Establishment Digest*, numbers 307 (March 1986) and 327 (December 1987), available from the Publications Sales Office, Garston, Watford WD2 7JR, telephone 0923 664444.

22 (section 2.7.2(B)) Deathwatch beetle infestations are very difficult to control. A four-page leaflet containing the most up-to-date advice is available, reference IP 19/86, from the Building Research Establishment, address as in Appendix entry 21.

23 (section 2.7.3) Ventilated chimney caps are referred to in Appendix entry 18.

24 (section 2.8.4) The Redundancies Officer of The British Institute of Organ Studies is David C Wickens, ARCO, 89 Blenheim Road, Cheadle Hulme, Cheshire SK8 7BB.

25 (section 3.5) The Empty Property Unit works in association with Shelter at 88 Old Street, London EC1V 9AX, telephone 01-253 0202.

26 (section 3.6) The National Council for Voluntary Organisations at 26 Bedford Square, London WC1B 3HU, telephone 01-636 4066, will also supply the addresses of Local Councils for Voluntary Service.

27 (section 3.7) The Rural Development Commission at 141 Castle Street, Salisbury, Wiltshire SP1 3TP, telephone 0722 336255, will supply the addresses of the appropriate county offices. Business in the Community at 227A City Road, London EC1V 1LX, telephone 01-253 3716, hold a register of Local Enterprise Agencies.

28 (section 3.8) The National Union of Townswomen's Guilds is at Chamber of Commerce House, 75 Harborne Road, Edgbaston, Birmingham, West Midlands B15 3DA, telephone 021-456 3435.

Acknowledgements

The information in this book is largely derived from meetings with conservation officers in many parts of England. I thank them for their numerous contributions and for making the research a pleasure by their enthusiasm and dedication to the cause of conservation. Amongst all those who helped me during the original research project in 1978–82, and also more recently, I particularly thank David Baker, Dean Clark, Stuart Fell, David Hanchet, June Hargreaves, John Harrison, Bob Hawkins, Christopher Hughes, Jeremy Jefferies, Barry Joyce, David McLaughlin, Anthony Pass, Mike Pearce, Peter Richards, and Chris Smith.

I thank all those who have taken time and trouble to show me buildings for possible case studies, including the buildings chosen, and to find old records and photographs.

The original research project, sponsored by the Historic Areas Conservation Division of the Department of the Environment, covered wider aspects of emergency repairs and included historic buildings records, buildings at risk, and local authority care of listed buildings owned by them. The information obtained from these studies has contributed to this book and I would like to thank all the English county councils and 45 district councils who supplied information and advice. In particular I thank the City of Bradford which allowed our practice to make a survey of all the listed buildings in their possession, many of which provided models of excellent continuing care.

I acknowledge with thanks the specialised information and expertise willingly contributed by many organisations and firms, including the Research and Technical Advisory Service of English Heritage, the Princes Risborough Laboratory of the Building Research Establishment, the Home Office Crime Prevention Centre, the Royal Commission on Historical Monuments, the Empty Property Unit, and the Redundant Churches Fund.

I thank Jean Marshall for preparing the drawings, and those members of the staff of English Heritage who have helped the progress of the book from research to publication and have finally edited and produced it.

My greatest thanks, as always, are to my husband Gordon for major contributions and proof reading at every stage. All the photographs not otherwise acknowledged were taken by him.

Index

Italicised figures are figure numbers, not pages on which figures occur; CS = case study.

access 21, 25, 26, 47, *10*
agricultural buildings, temporary use of 49
alarms 24, 30
anti-climb paint 29
amenity societies 11, 24
appearance of buildings *see* external appearance
archaeological interpretation 17
Architectural Heritage Fund 15, 56, 60
Arkwright, Richard 60
Arkwright House, Preston (CS 3) 60–3, *54–9*; causes of decay 60–1; emergency repairs 60, 61; full repair 62; quality of repairs 114
asphalt roofs 32, 117
assessment of buildings 17; of security 23
atmospheric exposure 12
awards 51, 56

balusters 18, 61
Barlborough Old Hall *25*, *31*
basements 18, 21
Bath Road, Cheltenham (CS 6) 77–80, 113, *82–7*; causes of decay 77–8; emergency repairs 78; full repair 79; quality of repairs 114
birds, exclusion of 20, 36, 40, *22*
Boat Museum *see* National Waterways Museum
Bolton Metropolitan Borough Council 73
Boshers (Cholsey) Ltd 51
Bradford: Hanover Square *36*; Preston Street *2*; Southfields Square *14*, *22*
brambles 41
Brandling Junction Railway 85
Brandling Station, Felling (CS 8) 85–9, *98–106*; causes of decay 87; costs of repairs 114; emergency repairs 87; full repair 87–8
brickwork 111,*29*, *138*
Bridger, Ann 55; Colin 51, 55
British Institute of Organ Studies 44
British Rail 81, 87, 113
Bromley, London Borough of 89, 94
Brown, Andrew 85
building materials, as cause of deterioration 12
bulges 42, *34*

Cabandale Ltd 51
Calne *37*
caretaking 23, 24, 46, 47, 49
Castlefields Urban Heritage Park 84
ceiling traps 36
ceilings 42, *32*, *33*
cellars 21–2, 25, 29, 35, 76
change of use 49–50
charitable trusts, grants 13
charities, as temporary users 47–9
Cheltenham Borough Council 77, 78; *and see* Bath Road, Cheltenham
chimneys 18, 31, 35, 36, 40, 91, 93, *31*, *111*, *115*
Civic Trust Commendation 51
cleaning of masonry 44, 84, 111, *137*, *138*
clocks 42–4, *35*
Clough, Robert 68
cocooning 36–7
commercial uses 49
community: assistance with security 23–4; use of buildings 50, 76, 89, 111
Community Enterprise Programme *see* Job Creation schemes
compulsory purchase 14
condition surveys 12
conservation 17–18; areas 13, 112, *44*, *135*; officers 11, 14, 17, 50, 70; teams 8, 14, 65, 113, 114
corbels *6*
cost of emergency repairs 114, 115; *and see* individual case studies
cracks *see* subsidence
Croal Irwell Valley 73, 75
Crompton, John 73
curtains 24

damp *see* water penetration
damp proof courses 34
deathwatch beetle 39–40, 118
debris *see* rubbish
demolition 105, 114
Derbyshire Historic Buildings Trust *4*
Derelict Land Grant 101
doors 18, 25–6, 36, 78, *16*, *52*
downpipes *see* rainwater systems
drains 34
drying out 35, 61
dry rot 22, 35, 38–9, 68, 70, 78, 94, 95, 104–5, 109

EEC regional aid 101
Elder Street, Spitalfields (CS 2) 56–9, 113, *44–53*; causes of decay 57–8; costs of repairs 114; emergency repairs 56–8; full repair 58–9; quality of repairs 114
electricity supply 29, 30
Ellesmere Port *see* Island Warehouse, Ellesmere Port
Ellesmere Port & Neston District Council 99, 101
emergency repairs: achievements of 114–15; costs of 114, 115; definition 8; quality of 114
Empty Property Unit 47
English Heritage, grants 13, 15, 19
Enterprise Trusts 50
external appearance 16, 24, 44, 45, 49, 84, 111, *36*, *92*, *137*, *138*

facades 79–80, 115
factories, temporary use of 49
Farnworth *see* Rock Hall, Farnworth
feasibility studies 17, 84
Felling *see* Brandling Station, Felling
felt roofing *see* roofs
fire 13, 29–30, 32, 36, 38, 61, 78, 99, 109
fireplaces 23, 29, 36, 59
Fitzgerald, R S 81
flashings 33
floors 18, 35, 36, 59
flues *see* chimneys
Folegate Street, Spitalfields *7*
Form Structures Ltd 61
Fort Knight Construction 89
foundations 19, 34
Friends of Arkwright House 60, 61–3
frost: damage 12, 34; protection against 38, 118
fungi *see* dry rot
furniture beetle *see* woodboring insects

gardens 45, 62, 89
gas supply 29
Gateshead Metropolitan Borough Council 85, 87, 89
Gillygate, York (CS 4) 63–72, *60–76*, 113; causes of decay 64–5; emergency repairs 65; full repair 65–6
glass 18, 20, 23, 29, *35*
Gloucester Docks, North Warehouse *8*
graffiti 25, 30–1
grants 13, 15; charitable trusts 13, 60; Countryside Commission 73; Derelict Land 101; DoE (non-outstanding conservation areas) 110; DoE Section 10 13, 51, 56, 60, 64, 65, 77, 89, 101; English Tourist Board 101; EEC Regional Aid 101; English Heritage 13, 15; Gillygate, York 65; local authorities 13, 45, 47, 51, 60, 77; Manpower Services Commission 60; Shell UK 101; Town Scheme 13, 64
Greater London Council 89, 92, 113
Greater Manchester Council 73, 81, 113
Greater Manchester Museum of Science and Industry Trust 81
Green Hill, Wirksworth *3*, *4*
ground movements *see* subsidence
gulleys 34
guttering *see* rainwater systems

handrails 18
Harden Old Hall, St Ives, Bingley *5*
Hardwick, Philip 89, 91
Hargreaves, June 64
Harrap, Julian 56
Heathcoat Street, Nottingham (CS 12) 109–12, 113, *135–40*; causes of decay 109; emergency repairs 109–111; full repair 112; quality of repairs 114
Hirst, Anthony 101
historic buildings: appearance *see* external appearance; choice of for case studies 113; definition for this book 8

historic buildings preservation trusts 15
housing, as temporary use 47

industrial uses 49
insects *see* woodboring insects
insurance 30, 61
Ironbridge *see* Maw's Tileworks, Ironbridge

Ironbridge Gorge Museum Trust 102, 105–6
ironmongery 18
Island Warehouse, Ellesmere Port (CS 10) 95–101, 113, *118–25*; causes of decay 99; emergency repairs 99–101; full repair 101
ivy 41, *30*

Jackfield Tile Museum 108
Job Creation schemes 65, 87, 88, 101, 106, 107, *132*
Johnson Richards Tiles 104
joists, and damp 36

Kay, John 60
keyholders 23, 30

Lamb Inn, Wallingford (CS 1) 51–6, 113, *38–43*; causes of decay 53–4; emergency repairs 51, 54–5; full repair 55–6; quality of repairs 114
Lancashire County Council 62
lead: gutters 33; roofs *see* roofs; theft of 23, 29, 78, 87, 94, *117*
leasing system 66
legislation, for urgent repairs 13–14
letter boxes 29, 116
lichens 41
lighting, external 25
listed buildings: legislation for repairs 13–14; *and see* minimum care
Liverpool Road Station, Manchester (CS 7) 81–5, 113, *88–97*; causes of decay 81; costs of repairs 114; emergency repairs 81–5; full repair 84; quality of repairs 114
Lloyds Bank, loans 60
local authorities: assistance with security 23; and clocks 43; historic buildings owned by 12; powers of 8; and short-life housing 47; *and see* grants; named authorities
Local Enterprise Agency *see* Enterprise Trusts
locks 24, 25–6
Lynam, Charles 102

maintenance 20, 34, 94, 95, 114
Manchester: City Council 81; Roundhouse Chapel *15*; *and see* Liverpool Road Station, Manchester
Manpower Services Commission 102; *and see* Job Creation schemes
Maw's Craft Centre 102, 108
Maw's Tileworks, Ironbridge (CS 11) 102–8, 113, *10*, *126–34*; causes of decay 103–4, 108–9; emergency repairs 104–7; full repair 107–8; quality of repairs 114
McMinn, W L 102
minimum care, of listed buildings 14, 16, 17, 114, 115
Moses Gate Country Park 73, 75
Moth, Ken 81
mouldings 18; temporary protection 42
Museums *see* Ironbridge Gorge Museum Trust; Jackfield Tile Museum; Museum of Science and Industry; National Waterways Museum
Museum of Science and Industry 82, *88*, *93*

National Council for. Voluntary Organizations 49
National Electricity Gallery 84, *89*, *94*
National Supervisory Council for Intruder Alarms 30
National Union of Townswomen's Guilds 50
National Waterways Museum 95–101, *118–25*
neighbours 24
Newcastle upon Tyne Liberal Club *27*
North Western Museum of Inland Navigation 99
notices 21, *9*, *121*
Nottingham: City Council 109, 110; Lace Market 109, 112, *135*; Technical Services and Planning Department 110; *and see* Heathcoat Street, Nottingham
Nottinghamshire Building Preservation Trust 109–11

organs 44, 118
outbuildings 25

painting 44
panelling 18, 23, 36, 57, 58, 60, 61, 62, 68, *49–50*, *58*
Pass, Anthony 73, 81
Pearson, Eric 64, 65
Penge *see* Royal Naval Asylum, Penge
Penty, W 72
permanent repairs 8, 16, 17, 92, 93, 113, 114, 115
Phillips, Niall 60
photogrammetry 17
photographic survey 17, 55, 68
Pillar Aluminium Ltd 77
planning consent 49, 54
plants 40–1, 109, *28*, *29*, *30*
plasterwork 42, *31*; *and see* ceilings
plinths 35
police, and assistance with security 23, 30
polythene 31, 37–8, 58, 61, 109
preservation trusts 15, 56, 57, 61–3, 109–11, 114
Preston Borough Council 60;*and see* Arkwright House, Preston

railings 21, 45
rainwater systems 29, 33–4, 81, 91–5, 100, *24*, *25*, *26*, *28*, *105*, *111*, *113*, *115*, *117*
record cards 9–11, *1*
recording 11–12, 17–18, 42, *1*
Regency architecture 77, 80
rendering 35, 42, *34*
rent 46–9, 66, 94
repairs: legislation 13–14; and temporary users 46, 47, 49; *and see* permanent repairs; individual case studies
Repairs Notices 14, 15
RICS/Times Conservation Award 51, 56
rising damp 34–6
Rock Hall, Farnworth (CS 5) 73–6, *77–81*; causes of decay 75; emergency repairs 75; full repair and conversion 75–6
roofing felts *see* roofs
roof spaces: fire risk 29; inspection of 31; use of 18; ventilation of 35, 117
roofs 31–3, *5*, *51*, *111*; asphalt 32; felt 31–2, 54; lead 32; security 29; slate 31, 81, 82–4, 97, *100*; tile 31, *51*; torch on 32; water penetration 31–4; *and see* rainwater systems, roof spaces, skylights, tarpaulins, individual case studies
Royal Naval Asylum, Penge (CS 9) 89–94, 113, *107–17*; causes of decay 89–91; costs of repairs 114; emergency repairs 91–4; full repair 95; quality of repairs 114
rubbish 21, 24, 29, 35, 36, 44, 45, 57, 58, 61, 65, 99, *14*, *31*, *72*, *105*, *120*
Rural Development Commission 50
rust 20

safety 18–23
scaffolding 19–21, 36, 37, 55, 58, 70, *7*, *8*, *41*, *48*
screening 37–8, *27*
sculpture 42
Section 10, grants *see* grants
Section 101 13, 78
security: of building 23–31, *24*; of stored objects 18; and ventilation 36; *and see* windows
settlement *see* subsidence
shops, as temporary users 47–9, *37*
shoring *see* scaffolding
short-life housing 47
skylights 25, 29, 61, 104, 105, *22*
slate roofs *see* roofs
smoking, and fire risk 30
South Oxfordshire District Council 51, 55
specialist teams 8
spiked collars for pipes 29, 116, *24*
Spitalfields *see* Elder Street, Spitalfields
Spitalfields, Folegate Street 7
Spitalfields Historic Building Trust 56, 57
stability 18–21
staircases 21, *10*
Stanley Partnership Cheltenham 77
Stock, Michael J 89
stonework 41–2, 77, 78, *25*, *85*, *86*
storage 18, 42, 58, 61, *117*
streetscape *47*, *53*, *72*, *74*, *75*, *76*; *see also* appearance; Gillygate, York
subsidence 12, 18–19, 61
support structures *see* scaffolding

surveys 12, 17, 18, 47, 55, 58, 68, 75, 78, 84

tarpaulins 32–3, 57, 61
Taylor, Charles Vernon 109
television aerials 21, 31
Telford Development Corporation 102, 104, 107
temporary use 46–50
tile roofs *see* roofs
tiles 18, 102–4
torch on roofing 32
Tower Hamlets, London Borough of 56
Town & Country Planning Act 1971 13–14
Town Scheme 12, 13, 65, 70
Town Teacher 89
traffic 21, 22, 54, *11–13*, *18*; schemes 64, 65, 109, 113
transport buildings, temporary use 49
Tyne & Wear Metropolitan County Council 85, 87, 89; Joint Conservation Team 85
Tyne & Wear Residuary Body 89

vandalism 12, 23, 24, 25, 44, 61, 75, 78, 99, 100, *14*, *15*, *22*, *57*, *100*, *120*
vegetation 24, 40–1, *28–30*, *86*
vehicles, damage by *see* traffic
ventilation 27, 35–6, 44, 105; and security 36
ventilators 35
volunteer workers 61, 100–1

Wallingford: Borough Council 54; Town Council 51; *and see* Lamb Inn, Wallingford
Ward Associates 89
warehouses *8*: Ellesmere Port 95–101, *118–25*; Liverpool Road Station, Manchester 81–5, *88–97*; Maw's Tileworks, Ironbridge 102, 107–8, *130–1*, *134*; temporary use 49
water penetration 12, 18, 31–8; damp proof courses 31; foundations 34; rising damp 34–6
water supply 38
Widecombe-in-the-Moor, Church House *26*
windows, security of 24–9, 37–8, 66, 105, 111, *17*, *18*, *19*, *20*, *21*, *22*, *23*, *65*, *80*, *102*, *106*, *130*, *133*, *137*, *138*
Wirksworth, Green Hill *3*, *4*
Wolstenholme, Thomas 66
Women's Institute 50
wood *see* dry rot; woodboring insects
woodboring insects 39, 40
workmanship, as cause of deterioration 12
Worthington, Thomas, and Sons 81
Wrekin District Council 102

York: City Council 64–5; Architects Department 64; *and see* Gillygate, York
Youth Opportunities Programme *see* Job Creation schemes